Young People, Citizenship and Political Participation

Young People, Citizenship and Political Participation

Combating Civic Deficit?

Mark Chou, Jean-Paul Gagnon, Catherine Hartung and Lesley J. Pruitt

ROWMAN &
LITTLEFIELD
INTERNATIONAL

London • New York

Published by Rowman & Littlefield International Ltd
Unit A, Whitacre Mews, 26-34 Stannary Street, London SE11 4AB
www.rowmaninternational.com

Rowman & Littlefield International Ltd. is an affiliate of Rowman & Littlefield

4501 Forbes Boulevard, Suite 200, Lanham, Maryland 20706, USA

With additional offices in Boulder, New York, Toronto (Canada), and Plymouth (UK)
www.rowman.com

British Library Cataloguing in Publication Data

A catalogue record for this book is available from the British Library

ISBN: HB 978-1-7834-8993-0
PB 978-1-7834-8995-4

Library of Congress Cataloging-in-Publication Data Available

ISBN: 978-1-78348-993-0 (cloth: alk. paper)
ISBN: 978-1-78348-995-4 (pbk.: alk. paper)
ISBN: 978-1-78348-994-7 (electronic)

♾™ The paper used in this publication meets the minimum requirements of American
National Standard for Information Sciences—Permanence of Paper for Printed Library
Materials, ANSI/NISO Z39.48-1992.
Printed in the United States of America

Contents

Preface

Mark Chou, Jean-Paul Gagnon,
Catherine Hartung and Lesley J. Pruitt

WHAT IS THIS BOOK ABOUT AND
WHY HAVE WE WRITTEN IT?

Young People, Citizenship and Political Participation: Combating Civic Deficit? is about the politics, citizenship and political education of young people in three Anglo-American democracies: the United States, the United Kingdom and Australia. We decided to focus on these democracies because they have each, especially in recent years, been claiming that there is a civic deficit among their young and because each country has tried to combat this deficit by renewing their civics education programmes. The central focus for policymakers and civics experts has been civics education in K–12 schools and the consistent inability of civics curricula to produce active, politically knowledgeable citizens who are wedded to the principles of democracy and who trust government, political parties, politicians and political institutions—or public authority more broadly.

Of particular concern among certain authority figures is a perception that young people are *not* participating politically, or that they are doing much less of this than older generations. It is this perception which has led in recent decades to the claim that young people's disengagement from politics, civic duty and the principles of democracy is leading to—or is already causing—a crisis of democracy.[1]

This logic, although appealing to certain mass media outlets and authority figures (which might help to explain why it has endured for so long despite its problems), has been heavily critiqued by academics for decades. 'What', to offer a few exemplar questions from this literature, 'is meant by young people'? 'Which civic duties and forms of citizenship are authorities advancing in one or more iterations of civics education'? 'Why is political participation seemingly limited to voting, joining political parties, legal petitioning and the indirectness of representative democracy'? 'What is a civic deficit and how is civics education meant to combat this'? Our book poses questions of similar tenor and contributes to this tradition of enquiry.

That said, we felt compelled to write *the book* because we wanted to explore a paradox in the literature. On the one hand are the claims that many young people are disengaging from politics and that this is 'bad' for democracy and on the other hand are the claims that many young people are engaging politically *in* or *through* their disengagement from 'conventional' politics and that this is 'good' for democracy. How can it be that these young people are both simultaneously 'bad' and 'good' for democracy? Does this affect citizenship? And what, if any, implications might this have for civics education today? We wanted to answer these questions, to dive in to the literature from our own points of scholarly expertise, to share with each other the evidence and arguments we have come across and to collectively write a book that will hopefully provide philosophical and policy insights into a discussion that is somehow both old and new.

WHAT IS DIFFERENT ABOUT THIS BOOK?

Writing *Young People, Citizenship and Political Participation* together gives this book an interdisciplinary character. Although we are each interested in young people, political participation, citizenship, civics education and democracy, and each of us comes from a social scientific background, we also have our own distinct research programmes. These colour the way we view the evidence and arguments upon which this book rests. Mark Chou's work has in recent years been interrogating certain large N surveys, like Australia's Lowy Institute Poll, and the claims these surveys have been making about the erosion of young people's faith in democracy.[2] But he also has been researching dramaturgy in political campaigns,[3] democratic meritocracy,[4] narratives of democracy,[5] democide[6] and other topics in democratic theory. Likewise, Jean-Paul Gagnon's work has been focusing on the philosophy of democracy,[7] adjectives of democracy,[8] non-human democracy[9] and the histories of democracies. Catherine Hartung's work focuses on the political sociology of children,[10] civics education[11] and the competing responsibilities of educating young people for global citizenship.[12] And Lesley J. Pruitt's work focuses on youth,[13] gender,[14] peacebuilding[15] and multiculturalism[16]—most recently culminating in a book on the United Nation's first all-female peacekeeping unit.[17] These different research interests combine in this book. We feel that it is this combination of interests that gives *Young People, Citizenship and Political Participation* its interdisciplinary character.

Another feature of this book, and something that is especially evident in the chapters to follow, is its emphasis on pluralism. 'Young people', 'democracy', 'citizenship', 'political participation' and 'civics education' are each understood as concepts that are plural in nature. This is what led us to argue that young people are often still being essentialised both in the literature that claims they are disengaged and in much of the literature that claims they are politically active. For instance, many scholars still speak of 'young people' as if they are a homogenous mass or of young people in binary terms—as either, or both, politically inactive and politically active. This demographic is far more diverse than much of the literature seems to suggest. There are *many ways of understanding* young people, democracy, political participation, citizenship and civics education. Our openness to, and engagement with, this pluralism affects the way we perceive issues like the supposed crisis of democracy that Anglo-American democracies are said to be experiencing or how young people are disengaging from/engaging in politics or how civics education can be reformed.

Our recognition of the pluralist nature of the main concepts in this book led us to recommend that policymakers and civics experts take up a particular form of co-design practice—a prescriptive point with which this book closes. We recognise that young people and their political practices are diverse, that there are many conceptions of democracy being practiced within the United States, the United Kingdom and Australia, that civics education has numerous iterations which carry with them their own (sometimes competing) normative values and pedagogical practices and that there is not just one form of citizenship but many forms of being a citizen, or a democrat, or just a person who happens to be living in a democracy. This sea of possibilities led us to ponder which policy design method might lead to a civics education that consistently reflects this plurality—and a civics curriculum that is meant to explore and debate different iterations of democracy, political participation, citizenship and civics education. This could be a type of schooling that might even lead young people and authority figures to come up with policy recommendations for pressing public issues together. This is why we settled on proposing co-design as a tool for policymakers and civics experts to use. We feel that this prescription is one of this book's more important features.

The last of this book's features is that it is written by young people. We are all in our early thirties. Although we do recognise the argument that youth is not simply about the number of days one has been on this Earth but is rather a state of mind,[18] this cannot discount or make up for the everyday lived experiences that we have each encountered as young people or for the fact that we *are* young and have been subject to different forms of age discrimination/marginalisation—especially in conventional politics. This fact adds a layer of solidarity to the book's purpose. It is not only about what we of course consider to be the important work of serious scholarly enquiry, and the advancement of discussion in what is a tremendously interesting field of research, but also about reflecting on our roles in this process. If those in control of reforming civics education were looking to involve young people, what level, degree or nature of participation would *we* expect? What kind of citizenship do *we* practice, which conceptions of democracy do *we* think we are advancing, how do each of us enact *our* politics? The solidarity feature of this book is that we are young people but also at the same time scholars trained to think critically about representative claims. We feel that it is this milieu in particular that promoted the unyielding pluralism which cuts across this book and which led us to settle on co-design—a hands-on and legitimate form of participatory governance—as a policy recommendation to use in the reform of civics education in Anglo-American democracies.

WHAT WE HOPE THIS BOOK WILL HELP TO ACHIEVE

It is our hope that this book will make a contribution to how young people's politics are perceived. Although it can be helpful, as a heuristic, to say that young people are either, or both, 'bad' and 'good' for democracy or simultaneously 'not participating' and 'participating' in politics, it still does not adequately reflect the stark diversity that is found among the young in the United States, the United Kingdom and Australia. A better truth is that young people are, like any other demographic, individuals with their own agency, who have their own unique sets of social, economic, political and cultural circumstances to deal with. Some young people celebrate certain conventional political practices, such as joining mainstream political parties (especially their youth branches) and prizing the vote. And they sometimes scorn their peers who do not do the same or hold similar values. Other young people are active online—they start and support petitions, participate in local through to global political events using social media and tweet at their MPs. Others take to the streets in protest when issues, like cost-cutting education reform, are tabled in parliament. Yet still more young people could not care less about any public issues or are for whatever reason ignorant about most of them. The confounder here, and it is something that we return to time and again in this book, is that a young person—or any person for that matter—can potentially be a mix of these practices and values and that this can change on an issue-by-issue or day-by-day basis. Although Bang and Sørensen do give us some footing in this sea of possibilities with their theory of the Everyday Maker,[19] it too is not immune from critique[20] as it does not capture the full extent of young people being, or not being, or half/ quasi being/not being, political.

We came to reflect on this perspective of young people's potentially endless political practices and values from a policy perspective. What tool could a policymaker, or civics curriculum expert, tasked with reforming and implementing civics curricula use to capture or reflect this diversity in their work? The answer that we settled on, which we point to throughout the book but really get stuck into in the final chapter (chapter 6), is the practice of co-designing civics education *with* a broad, representative, sample of young people—this should be something that recurs over a certain period of time so that civics curricula continue to reflect the political interests of the young. Co-design is a type of hands-on, shoulder-to-shoulder, process in which authorities co-produce an outcome with those people who are likely to be *most affected* by the outcome. If done correctly, co-design carries with it many goods-in-itself and is as such perceived by us—and a significant proportion of other scholars[21]—to be a legitimate and promising form of participatory governance.

Overall, we hope that this book will go some way to changing how young people are conventionally perceived and that this will lead those authorities responsible for forming civics education curricula in the United States, the United Kingdom and Australia, to take up the practice of co-designing civics education with a broad, representative, sample of their young people. Moreover, we hope that these authority figures will continue running this process every so often to help ensure that the civics curricula in Anglo-American democracies adequately reflects the interests of those who it is going to affect most—the young.

HOW THIS BOOK UNFOLDS

Young People, Citizenship and Political Participation can be understood as a book with two parts. The first part is more descriptive and explanatory. It consists of the first four chapters. And the second part, which is more normative and prescriptive, consists of the last two chapters. Chapter 1 provides a thorough overview of the issues at stake. It sets the scope and tone for the book. Chapter 2 shows how the link between the perceived political disengagement of young people and the crisis of democracy is riddled with logical inconsistencies. Chapter 3 surveys civics education and critically explains what its functions are meant to be. Chapter 4 gives a rich account of what young people's everyday political practices look like. That makes up the first part of the book. The second part opens with the penultimate chapter (chapter 5) which shows how competing priorities exist in the education of young people as global citizens. It reflects on this phenomenon and argues for the importance of a global citizenship education that incorporates these diverse and conflicting priorities. Chapter 6, the last chapter in this book, is where we make the case for co-designing civics curriculum with young people.

NOTES

1. Novak, A. (2016). *Media, Millennials, and Politics: The Coming of Age of the Next Political Generation*. London: Lexington Books. @ 172.

2. Chou, M. (2013). 'Democracy's Not for Me: The Lowy Institute Polls on Gen Y and Democracy'. *Australian Journal of Political Science* 48 (4): 485–494; Chou, M. (2015). 'The Rise of China and the Decline of Democracy in Australia?' *Australian Journal of International Affairs* 69 (6): 637–644; Chou, M., C. Pan, and A. Poole. (2016). 'The Threat of Autocracy Diffusion in Consolidated Democracies? The Case of China, Singapore, and Australia'. *Contemporary Politics* online first: 1–20.

3. Chou, M. (2012). *Greek Tragedy and Contemporary Democracy*. New York: Bloomsbury.

4. Chou, M. (2014). 'Projections of China's Normative Soft Power'. *Australian Journal of International Affairs* 69 (1): 104–114; Chou, M. (2016). 'Have the Black Knights Arisen? China's and Russia's Support for Autocratic Regimes'. *Democratization* online first: 1–11.

5. Chou, M. (2015). 'From Crisis to Crisis: Democracy, Crisis, and the Occupy Movement'. *Political Studies Review* 13 (1): 46–58.

6. Chou, M. (2013). *Theorising Democide: Why and How Democracies Fail*. London: Palgrave Macmillan; Chou, M. (2014). *Democracy Against Itself: Sustaining an Unsustainable Idea*. Edinburgh: Edinburgh University Press.

7. Gagnon, J.-P. (2013). *Evolutionary Basic Democracy: A Critical Overture*. London: Palgrave Macmillan.

8. Gagnon, J.-P, M. Chou, S. Ercan, and G. Navarria. (2014). 'Democratic Theories Database'. Available online: http://sydneydemocracynetwork.org/wp-content/uploads/2014/11/Democratic-Theories-Database.pdf; Gagnon, J.-P. (2016). 'Democracy's Adjective Pluralism'. Working Paper. Presented at the Australian Political Studies Association's Annual Conference, Sydney, 28 September.

9. Gagnon, J.-P. (2014). *Democratic Theorists in Conversation: Turns in Contemporary Thought*. London: Palgrave Macmillan; Gagnon, J.-P. (2015). 'Non-human Democracy: Our Political Vocabulary has No Room for Animals'. *The Conversation* December 21. Available online: https://theconversation.com/non-human-democracy-our-political-vocabulary-has-no-room-for-animals-51401.

10. Malone, K., and C. Hartung. (2010). 'Challenges of Participatory Practice with Children'. In B. Percy-Smith and N. Thomas (eds) *A Handbook of Children and Young People's Participation: Perspectives from Theory and Practice*. Abingdon: Routledge. pp. 24–38.

11. Hartung, C. (2011). 'Governing the "Agentic" Child Citizen: A Poststructural Analysis of Children's Participation'. Doctor of Philosophy Thesis, Faculty of Education, University of Wollongong. Available online: http://ro.uow.edu.au/cgi/viewcontent.cgi?article=4506&context=theses.

12. Hartung, C. (2015). 'Global Citizenship Incorporated: Competing Responsibilities in the Education of Global Citizens'. *Discourse: Studies in the Cultural Politics of Education* online first: 1–14.

13. Pruitt, L. J. (2008). 'The Drop Beats, Not Bombs: Music and Dance in Youth Peace-Building'. *Australian Journal of Peace Studies* 3: 14–32; Pruitt, L. J. (2011). 'Music, Youth, and Peacebuilding in Northern Ireland'. *Global Change, Peace & Security* 23 (2): 207–222.

14. Pruitt, L. J. (2013). *Youth Peacebuilding: Music, Gender, and Change.* Albany: SUNY Press; Pruitt, L. J. (2007). 'Real Men Kill and a Lady Never Talks Back: Gender Goes to War in Country Music'. *International Journal on World Peace* 24 (4): 85–106.

15. Pruitt, L. J. (2013). 'All-Female Police Contingents: Feminism and the Discourse of Armed Protection'. *International Peacekeeping* 20 (1): 67–79; Pruitt, L. J. (2013). '"Fixing the Girls": Neoliberal Discourse and the Girls' Participation in Peacebuilding'. *International Feminist Journal of Politics* 15 (1): 58–76.

16. Pruitt, L. J. (2016). 'Multiculturalism at Play: Young People and Citizenship in Australia'. *Journal of Youth Studies* 19 (2): 269–285.

17. Pruitt, L. J. (2016). *The Women in Blue Helmets: Gender, Policing, and the UN's First All-Female Peacekeeping Unit.* Oakland: University of California Press.

18. Clark, S. D., M. M. Long, and L. G. Schiffman. (1999). 'The Mind-Body Connection: The Relationship among Physical Activity Levels, Life Satisfaction, and Cognitive Age Among Mature Females'. *Journal of Social Behavior and Personality* 14 (2): 221–240. @ 225; Jönson, H., and A. Siverskog. (2012). 'Turning Vinegar into Wine: Humorous Self-Representations among Older GLBTQ Online Daters'. *Journal of Aging Studies* 26 (1): 55–64. @ 59.

19. Bang, H., and E. Sørensen. (1999). 'The Everyday Maker: A New Challenge to Democratic Governance'. *Administrative Theory & Praxis* 21 (3): 325–341.

20. Li, Y., and D. Marsh. (2008). 'New Forms of Political Participation: Searching for Expert Citizens and Everyday Makers'. *British Journal of Political Science* 38 (2): 247–272.

21. See, for example: Bauwens, M. (2009). 'Class and Capital in Peer Production'. *Capital & Class* 33 (1): 121–141; Certomà, C., F. Corsini, and F. Rizzi. (2015). 'Crowdsourcing Urban Sustainability. Data, People, and Technologies in Participatory Governance'. *Futures* 74: 93–106; Eversole, R. (2011). 'Community Agency and Community Engagement: Re-theorising Participation in Governance'. *Journal of Public Policy* 31 (1): 51–71; Misuraca, G., D. Broster, and C. Centeno. (2012). 'Digital Europe 2030: Designing Scenarios for ICT in Future Governance and Policy Making'. *Government Information Quarterly* 29 (Supplement 1): S121–S131. @ especially S122; Palmås, K., and O. von Busch. (2015). 'Quasi-Quisling: Co-Design and the Assembly of Collaborateurs'. *Codesign* 11 (3-4): 236–249.

Chapter One

Disengaged

Young People and Political Disengagement in Anglo-American Democracies

Mark Chou

Chances are, before she delivered her maiden speech in the British House of Commons on 14 July 2015, most Britons would have simply mistaken Mhairi Black for just another average twenty-year-old from Scotland. The newly elected Member of Parliament, who became Britain's youngest MP since thirteen-year-old Christopher Monck in 1667, barely looked the part. She was young and lacking in the polish of most career politicians. But that, it turned out, only made her comments all the more stirring. Using her speech to regale the chamber with stories from her constituency of Paisley and Renfrewshire South, on the southwest fringes of Glasgow, Black reminded her colleagues that the place she called home was shared with both legendary figures like William Wallace and a 'wonderful population with a cracking sense of humour'.

But these charms, as the Scottish National Party MP went on to say, do not hide the fact that 'it's not all fantastic'. For some time now, Black declared, life has been a struggle for many in Paisley and Renfrewshire South. 'We've watched our town centres deteriorate. We've watched our communities decline', she said to her fellow MPs in the chamber. 'Our unemployment level is higher than that of the UK average. One in five children in my constit-uency go to bed hungry every night. Paisley Job Centre has the third highest number of sanctions in the whole of Scotland'.[1] Her point was illustrated by a particularly poignant story of a man whom Black described as having been 'battered by life in every way imaginable'. With only enough money for a bus fare to the Job Centre or the local charity that fed him, she told the captive chamber that this man chose to go without food and drink for five days just to save enough money to travel to work. 'When he was on the bus on the way to the Job Centre he fainted due to exhaustion and dehydration', Black said. 'He was 15 minutes late for the Job Centre and he was sanctioned for 13 weeks'.

Is it right that something like this can happen in modern-day Britain? Is it right, Black asked, that the Chancellor has so easily abolished housing benefits for everyone below the age of twenty-one? What does it say about a government, a country, when the only young person who can access housing benefits in the United Kingdom is a twenty-year-old MP? As Black put it: '[w]e are now in the ridiculous situation whereby because I am an MP not only am I the youngest, but I am also the only twenty-year-old in the whole of the United Kingdom that the Chancellor is prepared to help with housing'.

Within a matter of days, tens of millions of viewers from around the world had logged online to watch the 'Baby of the House' deliver her maiden speech to Parliament. Trending as far away as Nigeria, the speech was even picked up in a spoof by well-known political satirist Amy Poehler while appearing on United Kingdom's comedy talk show, The Last Leg.

There are a number of possible reasons that explain why Black's speech went viral. For one, her gender has been a hot topic of discussion for some. For others, the fact that she's a Scot is important, particularly given the meteoric rise of the Scottish National Party (SNP) in 2015. As important as these reasons are, what had most people talking was Black's age or, more to the point, her youth. Only nineteen when she joined the SNP, Black now holds the title of the youngest British Member of Parliament for over three hundred years. She may not think of herself as a role model for young people in Britain, but many have come to see her as a representative for a generation of young Britons who are now facing some of the harshest social and economic conditions seen in decades. In the words of Benjamin Bowman, a British youth researcher, 'Black represents Britain's young people as they are. She comes from a working class family, she is a football fan and she has had her Twitter account pulled apart for swearwords and slang. She is articulate, intelligent and able'.[2] Her speech struck such a chord because it so perfectly described a reality that many young people in Britain have come to know all too well.

But there is another equally important reason behind Black's instant celebrity that is closely connected with her youth. Black is not only young; she is also political. Known to many as the 'SNP firebrand', Black's interest in politics was something instilled in her by her parents from a very young age.[3] For many political commentators, this sets her apart from her contemporaries. She is actively involved in community and party politics at a time when all we seem to hear is how young people in Britain and other Anglo-American democracies are disengaging from politics in droves. Rightly or wrongly, Black's celebrity is in part because she is the odd one out. To many, she is the symbol of everything today's youth are not: political, engaged and active.

A look at some recent trends confirms as much. There is now mounting evidence to suggest that unlike Mhairi Black, many young people in

Anglo-American democracies are not only disconnected from politics, they are also disinterested in it. The most worrying aspect of this disinterest has manifested itself in electoral participation. Looking at the recent voting patterns in Britain, the United States and Australia, for example, we see that more young people in the past decade or so have been abandoning the polls than in previous decades. Today, the young aren't voting nor are they participating in other arenas of formal electoral politics. On top of this, they're also turning their backs on mainstream political parties and movements. The result is that an increasing number of young people neither knows nor cares who their elected representatives are. All this shows that young people have abandoned the two main avenues of political participation as it has been traditionally defined in most democracies.[4] First, they seem to be no longer interested in conventional forms of participation, which ranges from voting to interest in party politics to engagement with interest groups. And second, fewer young people care to influence politics by petitioning their elected representatives and thereby taking part in the formal arenas of politics as defined by parties, parliaments and congress.

All this is capped off by several findings which suggest that some young people would even swap their democratic system for a non-democratic form of government if they could. A far cry from a Mhairi Black, who is both young and politically engaged, it seems today's youth are, to borrow the words of Pericles, the ancient Athenian democrat, 'useless' citizens who refuse to participate in public affairs.[5] It is of little wonder that politicians, policymakers, researchers and even popular culture have all portrayed the young as politically apathetic and lacking the necessary political knowledge[6] to uphold their democratic responsibilities effectively.[7]

Of course, it would be wrong to lay the blame solely at the feet of today's young. Voter turnout across all age groups has been declining in a number of Anglo-American democracies for some time.[8] As Simon Tormey has put it, 'The golden age of voter turnout was half a century ago, and since then we have seen a fairly steady decline in advanced democracies'.[9] But it is not just voting numbers that are on the decline. The other key measures political analysts typically look to gauge the health of a democracy—party membership, trust in politicians and the general interest a society has in politics—are also on a downward trend. It is a 'worldwide phenomena', argue Richard Niemi and Jonathan Klingler: 'declining trust and confidence in political institutions, lower respect for authority and its responsiveness to citizen concerns, and reduced political involvement' are trends visible not only in Britain, but in the United States, Australia, Canada and a raft of other so-called mature democracies as well.[10]

Whereas citizens in the Middle East and North Africa have been recently fighting for more democracy, their counterparts in North America, Western

Europe and Australasia seem to have given up on politics. To the vast majority of citizens within these democratic countries, politics and politicians
are dirty words, synonymous with other undesirable social goods, including corruption, greed and dishonesty. Today, as English political scholar
Matthew Flinders writes, citizens 'have become distrustful of politicians,
sceptical about democratic institutions, and disillusioned about the capacity
of democratic politics to resolve pressing social concerns'.[11] It is a sad truth
but democracies today are not sustained by the kind of healthy scepticism
which, for Flinders, they need to thrive. Increasingly, what drives citizens in
advanced Anglo-American democracies is a brand of corrosive cynicism that
is conducive to political suspicion, contempt and disengagement. Citizens are
giving up or at least giving into the sense that politics is hopeless.

It is against this backdrop that talk has turned in recent years to a so-
called crisis of democracy.[12] While certainly alarmist in nature, it is also true
that all is not well in the house of democracy. If the existence of electoral
democracy hinges on an engaged citizenry and a representative political
class that together work to keep government accountable and functional,
then everything we have talked about would suggest that there is a critical failure. Disengaged citizens, unrepresentative politicians, bureaucratic
morass—these are just some of the characteristics of democracy which commentators and everyday people use to describe politics in countries from the
United Kingdom to the United States. There is a palpable sense of a 'crisis of
actually existing representative democracy, a democracy that rotates around
politicians, elections, and parliaments', in Tormey's words.[13]

Fairly or not, young people are commonly singled out as the main culprits
of this contemporary crisis of democracy.[14] As is often pointed out, young
people's political disengagement today will have grave consequences tomorrow. After all, today's young will become tomorrow's citizens. What will
become of democracy when the future rests with a generation who have
become increasingly politically apathetic and disengaged? Is democracy not
headed for troubled waters when not insignificant numbers of 'millennials'
are so blasé about democracy that they would be willing to do away with it
for something better? 'From this perspective', writes Rys Farthing, it is easy
to think that 'a serious democratic deficit is imminent—the future of Western
democracy is under threat'.[15]

But to what extent are these assessments really accurate or complete? Are
young people turning away from democracy, or are these claims showing only
one part of the picture? What factors help explain their disengagement? And
what is to be done? We will answer these questions in this chapter by taking a
more in-depth look at the trends concerning young people's political engagement in three Anglo-American democracies—the United Kingdom, the United
States and Australia. In each instance, we look at the key reasons or factors

that help to explain why young people in particular seem to be disengaging from politics. But we follow up this discussion by asking the important though often overlooked question: are young people actually politically disengaged? This may seem an odd question to ask given all the claims we have already outlined in this chapter. We will go on to show that it is not. Finally, we will end the chapter with a brief discussion on how civics education can help bridge the chasm between disengagement and engagement among young people. Though this is something which will be taken up more fully in the chapters to come, we argue that involving young people in re-imagining a different approach to civics in schools is one important way of helping today's young to better understand the politics they practice and the political impact they already have, both in their own communities and farther afield.

YOUTH POLITICAL DISENGAGEMENT IN ANGLO-AMERICAN DEMOCRACIES

Whichever way you look at it, the claim that young people appear to vote less and care less about politics is hard to dispute. Younger people are on average less politically engaged than older generations. This trend is evident in many advanced democracies today, but here we want to focus our attention on the three Anglo-American democracies of the United Kingdom, the United States and Australia in particular—as recent scholarship shows that these countries have been and remain active in trying to address the problem of youth disengagement through their respective civics curricula (a point we will return to in this chapter). In all three cases, policymakers and scholars have been raising alarm bells for some time, warning against a potential democratic crisis as more and more young people disengage from politics.

In Britain, young people are frequently accused of being the culprits behind the decreasing voter turnout at national elections. According to Ipsos MORI research, in the space of a decade, youth participation in elections has seen a dramatic decrease. Whereas over 60 per cent of Britons aged 18 to 24 years were reported to have voted regularly in the early 1990s, by the 2000s this number had dropped to 40 per cent.[16] Public figures, from politicians to media commentators, have been quick to point fingers—particularly at the young. As Lucy Smith and Shelley Thompson write, '[t]he role of young people within British democratic life has caused concern and their noticeable absence in traditional forms of political participation continuously leaves them characterised as a "disengaged generation"'.[17] Increasingly, it is what the young are not doing—voting—that has become the greatest cause for concern.[18] In other words, British youth are now said to be the chief perpetrators responsible for Britain's civic deficit.

The problem, however, is not with all young people, just young people who have come of age in recent decades. Take the last two decades as an example.[19] In 1997, a not unhealthy 59.7 per cent of 18- to 24-year-olds turned out to vote in the British general election. But four years later, the percentage of young voters at the general election dipped well below 50 per cent—bottoming out at 39 per cent of eligible 18- to 24-year-olds. This downward trajectory hit rock bottom in 2005 when only 37 per cent of British youth voted at the general election. In 2010, there appeared to be a slight resurgence, with 44 per cent of the young voting. But even so, abstention among the young remained so high that, in the words of Bowman, had abstention been 'a party, 2010 would have been a landslide victory among the young'.[20] Finally, in the most recent election, held in 2015, we seemed to have returned to healthier levels of participation. Perhaps it was because the election was billed as a 'once in the generation' event that 58 per cent of under-25s graced the polls on election day. Despite still being much lower than the participation levels of older age groups, analysts were nonetheless reassured by the fact that the figure was at least closer to 1997 rates than the historic low recorded in 2005. This is no cause for relief though. In a review of electoral turnout among British young people in the period since 1992, Edward Phelps sees only a story characterised by a cycle of disengagement and disinterest.[21]

If we looked only at these numbers, then the conclusion is clear: in recent decades, British youth have been less likely to vote than their older counterparts, sometimes much less likely. According to policy analysts and curriculum experts, young people's rejection of formal political arenas and activities has much to do with their lack of political knowledge and civic responsibility.[22] As citizens, they are unable to understand why elections are important and why their participation matters. Instead, young people tend to feel unrepresented by politicians and mainstream political parties. With no vested interest in what takes place in the chambers of parliament, they then discard their civic responsibility to participate in politics. For civics experts, this cycle is a worrying one because political ignorance breeds distrust and distrust breeds cynicism, all of which leads ultimately to disengagement. In other words, when political ignorance goes unchecked, it will result in a civic deficit—and that is precisely what has occurred in Britain.

But why has all of this taken place in just the last two decades in particular? What has made young Britons socialised in recent times less likely to care about and participate in politics than those socialised half a century ago? The answer, as scholars have pointed out, has to do with generational differences experienced by young Britons who voted for the first time between 1992 and 2001 compared to those who voted for the first time prior to 1992. It is these generational differences which encompass the broader social and political changes witnessed in Britain during this period, which explain why today's young people have become more disengaged from politics during a time when there are paradoxically more avenues to participate than any time before.

Across the Atlantic, commentators have also been observing similar trends for some time. Writing in an American Political Science Association publication in 1997, Stephen E. Bennett made the point that as far back as the 1940s, research has shown young Americans to be 'less politically interested, knowledgeable, and active than those over 30'.[23] Youth political disengagement is not a new phenomenon, in other words. What is new, or at least different, is that whereas young Americans in the 1950s and 1960s tended to be more idealistic about politics and government than older generations, today's youth are, in Bennett's analysis, 'overwhelmingly cynical'.[24,]

The prominent American political scholar, William Galston, has made a similarly worrying observation. According to him, young adults who have just reached the age of majority are now less committed to the American creed—'an amalgam of constitutional democracy in politics, equal opportunity in the economy, and freedom in society'—than either their parents or grandparents were at a similar age.[25] Indeed, in the 1960s, some 60 per cent of young people were of the view that keeping up to date with political developments was important. By 2000, this figure had halved.[26] These findings have been a great cause for concern, and rightly so, since political disinterest tends inevitably to translate into political disengagement. And in the United States that is precisely what has happened. 'In 1972', writes Cheryl Russell, '53 percent of 18- to 29-year-olds went to the polls. By 2000, the figure had fallen to just 36 percent, a historic low'.[27]

The statistics on youth voting patterns have remained relatively steady in recent times according to studies conducted by the Center for Information and Research on Civic Learning and Engagement (CIRCLE).[28] For example, 51 per cent of 18- to 29-year-olds cast a vote in the historic 2008 presidential elections. By 2012, this figure had dipped six points to 46 per cent. While these numbers may not necessarily be considered as unhealthy, CIRCLE notes that it remains the case that half of the population aged 18 to 29 years consistently do not vote. Given that this demographic makes up 21 per cent of the voting eligible population in the United States, it means that 10 per cent of that population in America abstains from electoral participation on a regular basis. For no other reason, this is why youth political disengagement is an issue that deserves ongoing attention from politicians, policy analysts and curriculum specialists.

To conclude our snapshot of Anglo-American democracies, we turn to Australia. Examining Australia is important for several reasons. First, unlike Britain and the United States, Australia is the only advanced democracy in the southern hemisphere. It is geographically distant from North America and Europe and yet shares many of the same political customs and institutions characteristic of Anglo-American democracies. There is a second and maybe more significant reason for examining Australia. Unlike Britain and the United States, Australia is one of the few democracies globally that has compulsory voting. As such, one would expect it to be a stable and healthy democracy at least when it comes to electoral participation. And that is certainly true. But despite having much healthier rates of electoral participation than both Britain and the United States, Australian youth nevertheless exhibit many of the same tendencies and preferences as their northern hemisphere equivalents.

What is most worrying, as well-known Australian educator and sociologist Murray Print and Lawrence Saha demonstrate, is that a growing number of Australians aged between eighteen and twenty-five are rejecting their democratic responsibility when it comes to the vote. As they point out, '[w]hether these elections are national, state or local in nature, young people are increasingly avoiding voting'.[29] Even with sanctions in place, it seems many young Australians are refusing to participate in the democratic life of the country. While there are no hard and fast figures to go by, researchers have found that as many as half of young Australians would not actually vote if voting were not compulsory.[30]

But perhaps the most damning proof that young people in Australia are rejecting democracy has come in recent years from a series of annual polls conducted by the Lowy Institute for International Policy, a prominent Sydney-based think tank for policy and strategy. Over the years, the Lowy poll has uncovered a number of unexpected and concerning trends about the attitudes Australians hold towards key domestic and foreign policy issues. The finding that a significant proportion of Australians are largely apathetic towards democracy is certainly one of them. In the 2012 poll, for example, when the Lowy Institute first published findings on its democracy question, 60 per cent of respondents agreed that 'Democracy is preferable to any other kind of government'.[31] Twenty-three per cent, on the other hand, said that '[I]n some circumstances, a non-democratic government can be preferable'. Finally, a further 15 per cent of Australians responded by saying that '[F]or someone like me, it doesn't matter what kind of government we have'.

But that was not how the so-called Generation Y felt about democracy. Indeed, whereas 74 per cent of those in the age bracket of sixty years and over believed that '[D]emocracy is preferable to any other kind of government', only 39 per cent of 18- to 29-year-olds thought the same.[32] A further 37 per cent of Australia's youth held the view that a non-democratic government could be preferable under certain circumstances, leaving 23 per cent of Gen Y who either did not mind or did not care about the kind of government they had. In all, if we take the poll results at face value, close to two-thirds of the

Gen Y population in Australia are either indifferent or hostile to democracy. In the most recent poll, released in 2015, the figures somewhat improved. Despite this, close to 50 per cent of Gen Y respondents continued to think that either a non-democratic government could be preferable under certain circumstances or that it did not matter what kind of government they had.[33] Even taking into account the yearly variation, these polls would suggest that a sizeable proportion of Australians—especially in the 18- to 29-year-old age group—continue to remain sceptical about whether democracy is really the most preferable kind of government.

Understandably, these findings have caused a stir among Australian media, policy and academic commentators. For some, like former Lowy Executive Director Michael Wesley, they spotlight 'how lightly we take our democracy', something which comes as an unexpected surprise for him.[34] For others, like Chris Berg (2012), they are a clear vindication that we are now living 'in a profoundly undemocratic age', an age where '[w]e no longer have any faith in the capabilities of other Australians'.[35] These results 'should cause alarm', as Benjamin Herscovitch argues, and they should 'prompt soul-searching' for a country that has traditionally placed democracy alongside other uniquely Australian values like mateship, egalitarianism and a fair go.[36] Though scholars have long known that young people in Australia, as elsewhere, are increasingly distrustful of politicians and political institutions, and as such less likely to enrol and vote, few perhaps would have thought the situation so dire. But if the figures tell us anything then they surely tell us that Australian politics is in a sorry state. They are empirical proof that Australians, particularly young Australians, are now more willing to abandon democracy for other forms of governance should the perceived benefits outweigh the likely negatives.

EXPLAINING YOUTH POLITICAL DISENGAGEMENT

And so, there is now a situation where levels of youth political disengagement from formal democratic arenas is '[s]ignificant and increasing' in Print and Saha's words.[37] This is not just a problem affecting one or two democracies. It is widespread. Though we have only provided snapshots of three democracies in this chapter, what we have outlined here is representative of what is happening more broadly in Europe, North America and Australasia. For Print and Saha, there are three important conclusions to be drawn from these trends and figures.[38] First, young people in many advanced democracies no longer vote. They do not vote because they do not see it as an effective way of getting what they want. Second, though there may be the odd anomaly in this or that election, youth abstention from electoral participation is a fairly settled and widespread trend. Finally, from the perspective of politicians and policy analysts, voting is the most legitimate and important type of political participation for citizens to practice in a democracy. As such, not voting is indication that something has gone wrong. A democracy is only as strong as its demos. Those who do not vote do not support democracy.

But this is only scratching the surface of why the young have turned away from formal political practices. We may now have a clearer picture of what young people are not doing politically, but we still do not have a sufficient explanation as to why. In what follows, we want to briefly flag some of the most widely supported accounts offered by politicians, scholars and policy analysts to explain why the young are not voting and participating more broadly in politics. For the sake of clarity and brevity, we group these accounts into four broad categories of explanations: youth-focused, politics-focused, generational-focused and values-focused.[39]

Youth-focused explanations, on the whole, tend to analyse young people's political disengagement from the perspective of their age and social backgrounds. There are a number of factors researchers often examine in this context. For one, studies have found that the level of electoral participation can vary depending on the age of the first-time voter. Paradoxically, it is not the older first-time voters who are more likely to enrol and vote. Researchers have found that first-time voters who are sixteen or seventeen are significantly more likely to enrol to vote and participate in elections than first-time voters between the ages of eighteen and twenty.[40] Findings like this are important because they show that not only is age important but that youth is not always or necessarily anathema to electoral participation. Unlike those in the age bracket of 18–20, scholars believe that the majority of 16- to 17-year-olds have yet to experience the upheavals that come with leaving school, leaving home, finding employment and housing and adapting to life as young adults. Without these disruptions to life, younger teens therefore have more time and interest to vote. They may also be supported by a network of family, friends and teachers at home and at school, all of whom can help socialise them into the practice of voting at elections.

Contrast this with those in their late teens and early twenties. Many in this age bracket have left home and are without a fixed address, permanent employment or long-term considerations about money, marriage and home-ownership. With little tying them down, and no real thought for the long-term future, the incentives and logistics of casting a ballot are diminished.[41] In the words of one researcher, 'Young people [in their late teens and early twenties] do not yet have a stable basis for concern with politics and are more preoccupied with short-term projects'.[42] For these reasons, voting becomes a second or sometimes a third order concern.

Beside age, youth-focussed explanations also generally examine social backgrounds and educational factors when explaining why some young people tend not to participate in politics while others do. It is this range of factors that have given analysts and politicians a more nuanced picture of why some youths disengage from politics.

It has long been known that an individual's gender, class and education levels, among a range of other socioeconomic key factors, affects the likelihood of their participation at elections and other political events. As such, when studies tell us that young people as a whole are politically disengaged that is not exactly accurate.[43] Yes, young people on the whole tend to vote and join up to political parties less than older generations. But this does not mean that all young people are the same. When researchers ask the right questions, they have found that there is not one scenario but many which captures the political (dis)engagement of young people.

For instance, what is known is that generally young men will be significantly more interested in electoral and party politics than young women. Consequently, young men will vote and join political parties in numbers that far exceed young women. Moreover, those from middle-class backgrounds will have more incentive and capacity to engage formal political forums than their working-class counterparts. A young person from a middle-class family and neighbourhood will both perceive politics and politicians in a different light to a young person who has grown up in less-privileged conditions. It is these perceptions that will then influence whether they see participation in formal political arenas as practicable and effective. Finally, the level and length of an individual's education has been found to have a substantial effect on political participation. The more educated a young person is, the more they will care about politics and know how to participate effectively. The importance of education was confirmed in one study which showed that young people who did not graduate from high school are 50 per cent less likely to vote compared to those who did.[44] Interestingly, though, as Galston discovered in a separate study, despite the general increase in time spent in schools and at university, 'today's college graduates know no more about politics than high school graduates did 50 years ago, and today's high-school graduates are no more knowledgeable than were the high school dropouts of the past'.[45] This is an important point, and one which we will return to at the end of this chapter when we talk more explicitly about needing an age-appropriate and socially sensitive civics education.

Politics-focused explanations, the second category of justifications for youth political disengagement, tip things slightly on its head. Conventionally, the problem of youth disengagement has been approached from the angle of what young people are not doing. What is highlighted is the civic deficit that the young are principally held responsible for. Yet politics-focused explanations begin to ask a number of other questions. For instance, what role do politicians, political parties and the broader political system play in discouraging political participation among the young? Is it solely the fault of young people that they are not participating in politics, or is the way politics is done and covered also to blame?

Increasingly, it's been recognised that many young people are not 'apathetic' about politics; they disengage because they feel alienated from politics and the political process.[46] Rightly or wrongly, a large number of young people now have a dim view of politicians and mainstream political parties. In their view, those who populate Westminster, Capitol Hill or Parliament House care little about the plight of everyday young people—especially those from lower socioeconomic backgrounds. The young only become important to politicians if there is a political goal to be scored. Otherwise, they are simply ignored or condemned for their lack of civic engagement.

We saw a good example of this in Australia when Bill Shorten, the leader of the opposition, made a widely publicised speech in late 2015 about lowering the vote age.[47] Speaking about the challenges faced by today's youth—from the rising cost of education and climate change to housing affordability—Shorten confessed he was not at all surprised by young people's decreasing interest in politics. If government ignores the stark realities faced by Australia's youth, it's only natural that many will be disgruntled with the system. To 'tackle the apathy and cynicism of young people towards politics', the Opposition Leader said politicians must find ways to re-engage a generation of citizens who no longer seem interested in government affairs. Lowering the voting age to sixteen was, for him, a first step in that direction.

Though there is evidence to show that such initiatives can work when done in the right way for the right reasons, politicians from other parties quickly pounced on Shorten, claiming the only reason he proposed such a scheme was to capture the youth vote for his own Labor party. Knowing that young Australians tend to prefer Labor or the Greens to the ruling Liberal party, commentators dismissed Shorten's pitch as a mere political gimmick to help win himself more support. As a consequence, public debate in Australia quickly turned to speculation over Shorten's real motives and his desperate bid to win votes at the next election, possibly his last ditch effort to save his own job. These kind of schemes appear to young people as desperate and duplicitous. When debates about young people and politics take a turn in this acrimonious direction, even politically interested youth are likely to shun mainstream politics.

Politics-focused explanations cast a spotlight on such systemic biases and disincentives that together help account for why so many young people are choosing to abstain from participating in formal political activities today. These explanations are important because they demonstrate that not all young people are uninterested in politics nor think the act of voting in a democracy unimportant. Rather, it is that, despite their professed interest in politics and democracy, a significant proportion of youth nevertheless fail to exercise their right to vote. It is because of these systemic biases and disincentives that an active interest in politics in their everyday lives does not translate into active participation in formal political arenas, such as voting in elections.

Scholars have given a name to this phenomenon, and it's 'uncoupling'.[48] Uncoupling here has little to do with the love lives of Hollywood A-listers. Instead, it speaks more about a vital separation that has occurred in late modernity between politics as understood and practiced by 'laypeople' compared to the professional, arena politics now dominated by 'political authorities'.

In conventional accounts, politicians and political analysts have become known for lamenting the increasing political disinterest exhibited by the citizens they are meant to represent. Young people, in particular, bear the brunt of this criticism. When young people don't participate in politics, they are called slackers and blamed for instigating a civic deficit.[49] When they do participate, politicians label them delinquents because the way they participate is deemed as illegitimate. In the eyes of many political authorities then, young people more than any other demographic are not doing enough to fulfil their civic duties. When this happens, they are not only letting themselves down. They are weakening the system of representative democracy.

But this is just the perspective of the political elite. Ask young people themselves and you will likely get a very different view of what's been going on. Indeed, a common response researchers find when they do ask young people about political participation comes back to the theme of alienation. Young people express that they frequently feel alienated and let down by their so-called political representatives. What they care most about—social and post-material concerns—rarely rates a mention against the big-ticket issues contested at most modern democratic elections. How they choose to engage— through campaigns, social movements, online networks—is often condemned by political elite as illegitimate political participation. At its worst, therefore, some young people now no longer see what they understand and practice as politics *as politics*, which is something they believe is reserved for political leaders and representatives at Westminster or Capitol Hill. At its best, the young find little opportunity or incentive to participate in formal politics.[50]

There is thus a disconnect. The political system has become uncoupled from the young people it is meant to represent, just as young people have become uncoupled from the political system they are supposed to sustain. Political authorities only see what young people are not doing—and that is vote. Young people care deeply about issues which are political in nature. Yet they feel electoral channels are ill-equipped to redress them. For scholars,

understanding the phenomenon of uncoupling when it comes to political participation shows that a more holistic approach is required to understand why
young people are disengaging and what the political system itself is doing to
contribute to this.

Finally, politics-focused explanations can also examine the specifics of the
political system in which young people find themselves. Often studies about
youth political disengagement gloss over the impact particular political processes and voting systems have on electoral turnout and party memberships.
It is important to acknowledge that not all democracies are the same. Different
political systems will produce different levels of political participation.

A good way to illustrate this point is to compare the voter turnout in countries with different voting systems. For our purposes, we can use Canada and
Denmark. Both these countries are stable, advanced democracies. But there
is an important difference that sets these two democracies apart. Canada has
traditionally enjoyed low youth electoral turnout whereas Denmark has seen
a healthy majority of young people participate in national elections. Why is
this the case?

According to a study conducted by Jessica Nasrallah, the key difference
lies in their different political systems.[51] Canada (along with the United
Kingdom and the United States) has used what is known as the plurality or
first-past-the-post system for some time. As the world's oldest voting system,
experts often criticise the plurality model for producing wasted votes. In the
case of Canada, as Nasrallah describes, citizens will vote for their preferred
candidate or party in geographically defined districts. The candidate that
wins the most votes wins the district—even if they have not won the majority. The winner takes all in this system, whereas losers will have no say in
Parliament. Voting for outsider and unsuccessful candidates is thus a vote
wasted—because it makes no impact.

In Denmark, on the other hand, the system of proportional representation is used. In this model, seats are assigned to a party based more or less
on the proportion of votes they win. This is not only more representative; it
also enables more pluralism than what is possible under the plurality model.
The outcome, according to Nasrallah, is that a 'greater range of social representation is possible with a corresponding range of citizens' voices in a
political environment'.[52] For those who feel under-represented and ignored, a
proportional model provides more incentive to vote than the plurality model.
In Denmark's case, this has meant that even when young people express a
lack of interest in politics, they nonetheless tend to vote in much greater
numbers than in Canada. And so, a politics-focused explanation that takes
these considerations into account will perhaps be equipped to demonstrate
that youth political disengagement is not simply the fault of an apathetic and
uneducated youth.

ARE YOUNG PEOPLE REALLY
POLITICALLY DISENGAGED?

Our final two categories of explanations—*generational-focused* and *values-focused*—are best dealt with together. The reason for this is that both these explanations provide a more critical take on the situation. Rather than asking why young people are politically disengaged, they seek to question whether young people are in fact politically disengaged. As such, these final two categories of explanations shift the discourse from disengagement to engagement.

According to scholars who see generational differences as being an important determinant of how we understand and practice politics, it is often ignored that a person's political consciousness is shaped by their social and political experiences. These experiences, which are different for different generations in different places, determine what one sees as political and how one goes about doing politics. 'Each generation is consequently influenced by contemporary social and political events', argues Richard Kimberlee.[53] For today's young, who have grown up in an age where democracies produce a politics that is at once individuated, specialised, complex and cynical, it's only logical that their relationship with politics is different from that of their parents and grandparents.

Gerry Stoker, a British scholar of governance, has claimed that the individuated, specialised, complex and cynical nature of contemporary politics has considerable effects. As he puts it:

> The first means that people fail to appreciate the inherent collective characteristics of politics in an individualised world. The second suggests that politics is increasingly professionalised, leaving most of us in the position of being spectators rather than activists in any meaningful sense. Globalisation and technological advances tend to make politics even more remote because the complexity of the challenges they create mean political decision making appears to be beyond the control of everyday citizen activity. The fourth factor encourages a culture of hopeless fatalism about politics.[54]

These contemporary social and political conditions have shaped young people's view of the world—and the world of politics. In many instances, young people have known no other political reality. Acknowledging this starting point is important as it may lead to new understandings of why they do not vote, and why this may not necessarily be such a bad thing for them.

Indeed, for all the reasons Stoker outlines, disengagement from conventional formal political arenas may be less a negative than a necessity given today's political conditions. Typically, the issue of youth abstention is seen as a problem—a deviation by young people from the political norm where citizens are required to vote and ideally even care about politics. A generational account challenges this view. Rather than automatically seeing abstention as a problem to be solved, generational-focused explanations see what young people aren't doing as part of a broader (un)conscious effort to escape the corrosive cycle of alienation and hopeless fatalism that has come to characterise contemporary politics. In other words, disengagement when viewed through a generational lens can all of a sudden look quite different.

Simply put: the rejection of conventional politics—typically centred around elections, professional politicians, political parties and interest groups—may be giving some young people new choices and different political options. Of course, this is not to say that all young people who reject conventional politics are forging a new politics underpinned by their own 'lifestyle and non-materialist values'.[55] Some young people are simply uninterested in and apathetic about politics. And in these cases, youth-focused and politics-focused explanations may provide the more suitable means to redress the civic deficit. But alongside these young people are another group whose abstention is a more active response to contemporary political conditions. To enact their politics, voting at elections no longer takes centre stage. While voting at elections, joining a political party and petitioning a Member of Parliament do not become irrelevant, neither are these political acts sacralised. Where they are relevant and effective, they will be preferred. Where they are not, it is not out of the question to abstain, protest, boycott, sign petitions, culture jam, organise community rallies or hit the Twittersphere. All these are ways of doing a 'new politics' said to 'reflect young people's generational concerns, lifestyles and value orientations'.[56]

These two categories of explanations thus appreciate that the issue of youth political disengagement is a matter of perspective. Young people are certainly abandoning formal political arenas and avenues of participation. Yet this is only one side of the coin; one particularly narrow way to see things. There is a reason, many in fact, why young people are abandoning formal politics—beyond the typical accusations that they are lazy, self-interested and apathetic. If we look at what is happening from a different perspective, it is possible to see beyond the image of a lazy, self-interested and apathetic generation. While this depiction is certainly true of some young people, it does not represent the many who, feeling alienated from the political system, are compelled to abstain from formal political arenas or to participate on their own terms.

As youth researchers Anita Harris, Johanna Wyn and Salem Younes have put it, more young people than ever are refusing to participate in formal politics.[57] However, only rarely is this because of their so-called political apathy. The more likely scenario is that having sought and been denied inclusion in formal political forums, they are now looking elsewhere. 'Given their sense of exclusion from formal politics', write Harris and Wyn, 'young people are obliged to seek out alternative forums and alternative discourses for the expression of political points of view'.[58] And this is the point: apathy certainly plays a part in explaining youth disengagement from politics. Yet its part is often much smaller than analysts and politicians would have us believe. Rather than always talking about apathy, and its corollary civic deficit, we perhaps need to pay equal attention to alienation, and its corollary disenchantment.[59] It is the latter, rather than the former, which will help account both for youth disengagement from formal political arenas and their turn to informal political practices.

Alienation and disenchantment also helps explains something else. Before political habits form and we begin to conform, people are more likely to experiment and challenge political conventions. Younger people tend to take more risks and test for themselves what works and what does not. When they realise that something is making no impact, they are more likely than older people to change course and try something new. The same is true for politics. Young people who have experienced the politics of the ballot box generally come away disappointed. What is more, they are often left with a sense that their engagement has made minimal difference—particularly to issues they care most about. They know that most political leaders do not need their participation to win elections. As such, what they do—and sometimes refuse to do—is driven by what works for them.

It is for this reason that more and more young people are favouring what is known as a cause-oriented style of politics than older generations, many of whom have already been socialised into doing politics a particular way. It is important to realise here that cause-oriented politics is not a one-size-fits-all approach to political participation. Cause-oriented politics is defined by the particular cause or concern. The cause determines the type of politics and participation employed. Voting and joining mainstream political parties will be preferred when the objective is to engage politicians and affect change within the existing political system. Abstention is the choice of those who do not care or do not wish to contribute to a political system in which they have little influence. For those wanting direct action, protests and demonstrations will be the method of choice. Ethical buying and boycotts will benefit those who want their daily consumption practices to make a statement. These are but a few of the many and varied ways to participate, ranging from campaigning, volunteering to online forums. What matters to practitioners of this cause-oriented politics is not a rigid adherence to one type of politics or political participation, but the flexibility to choose multiple, sometimes contradictory, political concerns and practices.

Despite its flexibility though, there are at least three important unifying traits evident in cause-oriented politics. Understanding these traits will also help us understand how many contemporary young people are conceptualising the political today. The first trait is one often spoken about by scholars when referring to the politics of young people: the shift from a materialist to post-materialist political agenda.[60] Simply stated, the claim here is that younger people have a tendency to be interested in more than personal wealth and security. While these issues are no doubt important, more young people have said when asked by researchers that their passions extend to a range of other causes, from climate change, the plight of refugees, unequal global development, as well as local community issues. What this signifies, according to scholars, is that young people exhibit a greater propensity to care more about post-materialist issues that are not determined by the bottom dollar than older generations. Again, this is not to generalise: not all young people hold these views. Still, there is a noticeable number of youth who now value quality of life issues and care about the longer-term effects of society's consumption practices. These concerns shape their activism, which in turn become as eclectic as their various interests.[61]

A second political trait of cause-oriented politics relates to the status of the state. For much of the twentieth century, the state was the key political reference point for everyday citizens and their political activities. We voted, joined political parties, took part in political campaigns because we cared about what was happening within our own countries. We chose presidents and prime ministers based on their vision for our country's future. Voting at national elections, in this regard, is both natural and essential if we want to influence the course the state takes. It is also part of our national civic duty. Increasingly, though, young people's political agenda are no longer, or not strictly, tied to the state. The state is only one of many possible political battlegrounds. From the local to the global, there are now many important realms that young people's concerns encroach upon.

To this end, because the issues young people care about have no single, fixed reference point, simply voting at national elections is no longer politically sufficient. Alongside government, political activity and activism has to be directed towards NGOs, MNCs, social movements and other interest groups. To do this effectively, a range of other forms of political participation becomes necessary, from political consumerism, e-democracy, self-governance, to active disengagement.[62] Those who engage in this type of politics have commonly been referred to as Everyday Makers; their political participation is dictated less by the state than their own terms. As the British political scientists Yaojun Li and David Marsh argue, 'Everyday Makers do not feel defined by the state; they are neither apathetic about, nor opposed to, it'.[63] Most important, as Li and Marsh stress, 'Everyday Makers typically think globally, but act locally. They have no interest in producing a new form of interest representation and have minimal interest in party politics'.

Increasingly, it is this type of everyday politics that youth researchers believe has come to define young people's cause-oriented political engagement.

The third and final political trait of cause-oriented politics can either be viewed as distinct from or a subset of the first two traits. According to youth sociologist Rys Farthing, politicians and analysts have generally responded to the declining engagement with politics by young people by portraying them as either apathetic or part of a generational vanguard forging a new type of politics.[64] But for Farthing, there is another way or paradigm through which to portray what young people are doing. This is the vision of a radically unpolitical youth.

Drawing on Ulrich Beck's concept of the risk society, Farthing makes the case that 'young people's rejection of politics is their way of negotiating the new freedoms of a risk society'.[65] What is often missed or misunderstood is that young people are not disengaging from politics because they lack the civic imperative; it is more that they have an entirely new civic imperative made necessary in the new form of society they inhabit. Young citizens, Farthing points out, '*live* their politics—they do not vote for change; they do change'.[66] If this is the case, then a refusal to do something is not apathy but an immense, perhaps the 'deepest challenge' one can front in response to something.[67] For Farthing, it is important to view the rise of a radically unpolitical youth less as a corollary of their disengagement than 'the core of their political action'. The cause of their politics is the rejection of formal politics.

What we can take away from these three traits, and the cause-oriented politics that is encapsulated by them, is this: young people are rejecting, refining as well as revolutionising politics. Those wanting a clear picture or a single paradigm with which to define and understand youth political (dis) engagement may be disappointed. Whereas some young people are simply just disengaged from politics, others are at the vanguard of an unconventional type of politics and political participation that as yet is not fully understood. Then there are those whose politics and political activism falls somewhere between these two extremes. As Bowman rightly reminds us, the young are now 'voters, but also abstainers, protestors, organisers, union members and ethical buyers'.[68] If there is in fact one thing that they do show us then it is that there is not one way to do politics. There are many.

But diversity can create its own problems. Because there are now so many ways of doing politics and becoming political, definitions become essential. Without giving meaning to one's politics and political participation, there is a risk that it will be defined or ill-defined by someone else. There is need for young people to take a lead in defining their own politics. Young people, as some scholars have stressed, must have a voice in articulating 'how they conceive of politics, what it means to them and how they relate to it'[69]—or risk politicians, curriculum experts and policy analysts doing it for them.

Unfortunately, this is a task that is easier said than done.[70] It's one thing to do something. It's quite another to conceptualise and communicate what one is doing to a broader community. Part of the problem here goes back to the issue of uncoupling. Youth have 'very little language with which to conceive of their everyday issues as belonging to the same arena of politics' as that which is populated by professional politicians and mainstream political parties.[71] At its worst, some young people do not even see what they understand and practice in their own communities *as* politics. Politics, for them, is something largely reserved for political elites in Westminster, Washington or Canberra. As Harris and Wyn have put it, '[p]olitics is seen to occupy a particular formal, public space which is not part of youth geographies'.[72] When this happens, is it any wonder that young people are 'forced into a narrow, individualised conceptualisation of their key concerns as belonging to a personal space, one that is separated off from politics'?

COMBATING CIVIC DEFICIT, DEFINING CIVIC SURPLUS

But what can be done to 'recouple' young people with the political system and vice versa? How can young people themselves help fight the perception of a civic deficit? Where can young people look to find the language—their own language—to enable them to articulate the civic surplus they have given rise to? What can educators and policymakers do to aid young people to bridge the chasm separating the popular discourses of disengagement from the type of cause-oriented political practices they have adopted?

The answer that we will propose in this book has to do with a critical re-evaluation of how civics and citizenship are conceived and taught in schools. This solution may sound rather conventional, and certainly it can be. Widely considered by politicians and educators in advanced democracies as the solution for youth political disengagement, civics education has in reality rarely ever been more than a Band-Aid solution at best. At its worst, civics programmes have been costly government initiatives that have had little to no impact on how young people approach politics. Pedagogically, normatively and practically, they have underscored the civic deficit discourse and helped to further legitimise formal political practices.

Far from condoning a conventional approach to civics, our proposal is based on a case that young people must be incorporated into debates about civics implementation and teaching practices. A civics education that is for young people needs to incorporate the voices and realities of the young—the disengaged, alienated, the abstainers and the radically engaged. Politicians, curriculum experts and stage of schooling specialists can only achieve a fuller understanding of youth political (dis)engagement when they draw on the lived experiences of the young. Otherwise, youth-oriented policies decided by an ageing political elite risks further marginalising and misrepresenting the needs of young people.

Whatever one's view of existing civics education programmes, it is hard to dispute that in theory an education in civics is one important avenue to raise and nurture political awareness in our young. Without such an education, scholars have argued, 'we cannot expect to see a fully engaged young generation and an in-depth critical discourse analysis of media texts'.[73] For Galston, civics education can foster civic knowledge, which can lead to more enlightened self-interest, support for democratic values and an increased quality of political participation.[74] Civics education is thus integral to an 'education for democracy'.[75] Through it, young people can

> acquire meaningful knowledge about the political and economic system, to recognize the strengths and challenges of democracy and the attributes of good citizenship, to be comfortable in participating in respectful discussion of important and potentially controversial issues, and to be aware of civil society organizations. Knowledge should lead to both skills in interpreting political communication and to dispositions favouring actual involvement in conventional citizenship behavior, especially voting on the basis of the candidates' issue positions.[76]

Such a view is premised on the assumption that a well-functioning representative democracy depends on citizens who are both informed of and active in the mechanisms of representative democracy.

Consequently, for both political scientists and civic educators, there is a commonly held conviction that if young people are taught the basic tenets of citizenship, democracy and the political institutions that govern them, they will not only be more politically savvy. They will also realise that it is in their best interest to actively participate in politics. After all, as Kevin Chin and Carolyn Barber point out, civics is about enabling youth to engage 'meaningfully in public affairs'.[77] Indeed, it was the belief that an education in civics could positively overcome the 'decline in civic engagement, political efficacy, and in the capacity of citizens to organize themselves' that led an organisation like the American Political Science Association to create the Task Force on Civic Education for the Next Century in 1996.[78]

But the reality is never so simple. Civics education may sound ideal in theory, yet implementation and practice are another matter. Indeed, debates about what an education in civics and citizenship should encompass are contentious issues. As Wayne Ross argues, there may be 'widespread agreement that the appropriate aim of . . . "citizenship education" [is] the preparation of young people so that they possess the knowledge, skills, and values necessary for active participation in society'.[79] Yet what there is not, according to Ross,

is 'consensus on what "citizenship" means, nor on the implications of democratic citizenship for curriculum and instruction'. Joel Westheimer and Joseph
Kahne concur. For them, educators are no different from activists, politicians
and scholars in that they do not all share one understanding of citizenship and
democracy. The 'various perspectives on citizenship', when translated to civics, will therefore 'have significantly varying implications for curriculum'.[80]
Different programmes produce different outcomes, different forms of political participation and even different types of citizens.

The reason for this, argue Cosmo Howard and Steve Patten, is simple.[81]
'Our visions of civics education are shaped by the way democracy is defined',
they point out. Notions of civicism and democracy are not universal but influenced 'by our views on the boundaries of politics, our understanding of the
social processes and forces that determine the distribution of political power
and our understanding of the meaning, rights and obligations of democratic
citizenship'.

Yet all this talk of civics and citizenship frequently shrouds another problem endemic to discussions about civics education in advanced democracies.
What problem is that? Simply put, it is that young people themselves have no
say—and are rarely consulted—when civic and curriculum experts discuss
what type of civics education and notion of citizenship should be taught to
young people. Unlike expert educators, political analysts or adult laypeople,
young people have been excluded from these important debates because they
are deemed to lack the appropriate knowledge and experience. After all, it is
their lack of civic knowledge and experience that makes civics education necessary. All this is backed by developmental theories which tell us that young
people are limited in what they know and understand. They have yet to grasp
the complex realities of life and consulting them on such matters would be
a disaster waiting to happen. As Farthing writes, the conservative critique of
involving young people in debates about civics education stresses that 'the
valorisation of young people's knowledge and input is at best naïve, and at
worst damaging'.[82]

But our book will seek to reframe the argument. Our key claim is that
young people have a depth of knowledge, experience and practice that could
potentially revitalise how civics is conceived and taught. Consulting them
about this knowledge, experience and practice can not only make for a more
reflective civics experience; it will broaden the curricula. When this is done, a
civics curriculum has a greater chance of speaking to the realities of the actual
young people whose view of politics it is hoping to shape. Such a process can
shift youth consultation practices away from the 'tokenism of current political
processes that provide little sense of connection between acts of consultation
and higher level decision-making by politicians and policymakers who have
little knowledge about young people's lives' (Harris and Wyn 2010).

Ultimately though, our argument is that civics education can act as a crucial link between the two key discourses of youth political disengagement and the type of cause-oriented politics being spearheaded by many young people today. Yet for more young people to move from the former discourse to the latter, they actually need to feel that the civics education they receive is representative of their diverse realities and the 'multiplicity of young people's political participation—including acknowledgement of the capacity of new agendas, spheres and forms, and the deep significance of disengagement'.[83] Who better to consult about these new agendas, spheres and forms of political (dis)engagement than young people themselves? What better way for youth to take greater ownership and pride in their own politics than being part of discussions on how they should be educated about civics and citizenship? These are the questions that the following chapters will seek to answer.

NOTES

1. A sanction in Scotland is when an unemployed person's social benefits are withheld for a period of time, often as a penalty, for breaching one or more of the rules found in the state's employment programme.

2. Bowman, B. (2015). 'Mhairi Black goes viral: How Britain's youngest MP became a political star'. *The Conversation*. Online 16 July 2015.

3. Cramb, A. (2015). 'Meet Mhairi Black, Britain's youngest MP for 350 years, and an SNP firebrand'. *The Telegraph*. Online 8 May 2015.

4. McCaffrie, B. and S. Akram (2014). 'Crisis of democracy? Recognizing the democratic potential of alternative forms of political participation'. *Democratic Theory*. **1** (2): 47–55.

5. Bennett, S. E. (1997). 'Why young Americans hate politics and what we should do about it'. *PS: Political Science and Politics*. **30** (1): 47–53. @ 50.

6. Rapeli, L. (2014). 'What should the citizen know about politics? Two approaches to the measurement of political knowledge'. *Democratic Theory*. **1** (1): 58–93. @ 64 onwards.

7. Farthing, R. (2010). 'The politics of youth antipolitics: Representing the "issue" of youth participation in politics'. *Journal of Youth Studies*. **13** (2): 181–195. @ 182.

8. Dalton, R. J. (2008). 'Citizenship norms and the expansion of political participation'. *Political Studies*. **56** (1): 76–98. @ 92.

9. Tormey, S. (2014). 'The contemporary crisis of representative democracy'. *Democratic Theory*. **1** (2): 104–112. @ 105.

10. Niemi, R. G. and J. D. Klingler (2012). 'The development of political attitudes and behaviour among young adults'. *Australian Journal of Political Science* **47** (1): 31–54. @ 31–32.

11. Flinders, M. (2012). *Defending politics: Why democracy matters in the twenty-first century*. Oxford: Oxford University Press. @ 1–2.

12. Tormey, S. (2015). *The end of representative politics.* Cambridge, Polity Press; Ercan S. A. and J.-P. Gagnon. (2014). 'The crisis of democracy: Which crisis? Which democracy?' *Democratic Theory* **1** (2): 1–10; Runciman, D. (2013). *The confidence trap: A history of democracy in crisis from World War I to the present.* Princeton: Princeton University Press.

13. Tormey, S. (2014). 'The contemporary crisis of representative democracy'. *Democratic Theory* **1** (2): 104–112. @ 106.

14. Farthing, R. and A. Hudson (2015). 'What would make young people get interested in politics?' *New Statesmen*. Online 9 April 2015.

15. Farthing, R. (2010). 'The politics of youth antipolitics: Representing the "issue" of youth participation in politics'. *Journal of Youth Studies*. **13** (2): 181–195. @ 183.

16. Ipsos MORI. (2015). *'Political and social trends'.* Online 15 December 2015; Sloam, J. (2015). 'How did young people vote in 2015, and what does it mean for the future?' *The Conversation*. Online 15 May 2015.

17. Smith, L. and S. Thompson (2015). 'Tuning out or tuned out? A critical discourse analysis of youth political participation in Britain'. *Journal of Promotional Communications*. **3** (2): 295–301. @ 295.

18. Evans, G. (2015). 'Play fair with young people, George Osbourne—let 16-year-olds vote'. *The Guardian*. Online 22 July 2015.

19. See Smith, L. and S. Thompson (2015). 'Tuning out or tuned out? A critical discourse analysis of youth political participation in Britain'. *Journal of Promotional Communications*. **3** (2): 295–301. @ 295; Evans, G. (2015). 'Play fair with young people, George Osbourne—let 16-year-olds vote'. *The Guardian*. Online 22 July 2015; 'Why young people don't vote'. *The Economist.* Online 29 October 2014; Henn, M., M. Weinstein and S. Forrest. (2005). 'Uninterested youth? Young people's attitudes towards party politics in Britain'. *Political Studies* **53** (3): 556–578. @ 556.

20. Bowman, B. (2015). 'Hate the players, love the game: why young people aren't voting'. *The Conversation*. Online 30 April 2015.

21. Phelps, E. (2012). 'Understanding electoral turnout among British young people: A review of the literature'. *Parliamentary Affairs*. **65** (1): 281–299.

22. Qualifications and Curriculum Authority (1998). *Education for citizenship and the teaching of democracy in schools: Final report of the Advisory Group on Citizenship (Crick Report)*. London: QCA.

23. Bennett, S. E. (1997). 'Why young Americans hate politics and what we should do about it'. *PS: Political Science and Politics*. **30** (1): 47–53. @ 48.

24. Ibid. @ 50.

25. Galston, W. A. (2007). 'Civic knowledge, civic education, and civic engagement: A summary of recent research'. *International Journal of Public Administration*. **30** (6–7): 623–642. @ 624.

26. Ibid. @ 629.

27. Russell, R. (2012). 'The surprising trends that suggest young people won't vote in 2012'. *New Republic*. Online 15 February 2012.

28. 'Youth Voting'. *The Center for Information and Research on Civic Learning and Engagement*; *all together now: Collaboration and innovation for youth engagement: The Report of the Commission on Youth Voting and Civic Knowledge*. (2013). Medford, Center for Information and Research on Civic Learning and Engagement.

29. Print, M. and L. Saha (2007). 'Youth, democracy and politics: Issues in Australia'. in Saha, L., M. Print and K. Edwards (eds.). *Youth and political participation*. Rotterdam: Sense Publishers. @ 1.

30. Martin, A. (2012). 'Political participation among the young in Australia: Testing Dalton's Good Citizen Thesis'. *Australian Journal of Political Science*. **47** (2): 211–226. @ 212.

31. Hanson, F. (2012). *The Lowy Institute Poll 2012: Australia and New Zealand in the world.* Sydney: Lowy Institute for International Policy. @ 13.

32. Ibid. @ 13–14.

33. Oliver, A. (2015). *The Lowy Institute Poll 2015.* Sydney: Lowy Institute for International Policy. @ 15.

34. Callick, R. and S. Gosper (2015). 'What's democracy done for me lately, asks Gen Y'. *The Australian*. Online 5 June 2012.

35. Berg, C. (2012). 'Politics of contradiction mean democracy for me, but not for thee'. *Sydney Morning Herald*. Online. 10 June 2012

36. Herscovitch, B. (2012). 'Why democracy is a victim of its own success'. *Canberra Times*. Online 28 June 2012.

37. Print, M. and L. Saha (2007). 'Youth, democracy and politics: Issues in Australia'. in Saha, L., M. Print and K. Edwards (eds.). *Youth and political participation*. Rotterdam, Sense Publishers. @ 1.

38. Ibid.

39. Kimberlee, R.H. (2002). 'Why don't British young people vote at general elections?' *Journal of Youth Studies*. **5** (1): 85–98.

40. Zeglovits, E. and J. Aichholzer (2014). 'Are people more inclined to vote at 16 than at 18? Evidence for first-time voting boost among 16- to 25-year-olds in Austria'. *Journal of Elections, Public Opinion and Parties*. **24** (3): 351–361.

41. Russell, R. (2012). 'The surprising trends that suggest young people won't vote in 2012'. *New Republic*. Online 15 February 2012.

42. Quintelier, E. (2007). 'Differences in political participation between young and old people'. *Contemporary Politics*. 13 (2): 165–180. @ 169.

43. Henn, M. and N Foard (2014). 'Social Differentiation in young people's political participation: the impact of social and educational factors on youth political engagement in Britain'. *Journal of Youth Studies*. **17** (3): 360–380.

44. Bastedo, H. (2015). 'Not "one of us": Understanding how non-engaged youth feel about politics and political leadership'. *Journal of Youth Studies*. **18** (5): 649–665.

45. Galston, W. A. (2007). 'Civic knowledge, civic education, and civic engagement: A summary of recent research'. *International Journal of Public Administration*. **30** (6–7): 623–642. @ 630.

46. Stoker, G. (2006). 'Explaining political disenchantment: Finding pathways to democratic renewal'. *The Political Quarterly*. **77** (2): 184–194.

47. Chou, M., C. Hartung and J.-P. Gagnon (2015). 'Shoten's plan to lower the voting age could help increase political engagement'. *The Conversation*. Online 2 November 2015.

48. Henn, M. and M. Weinstein (2006). 'Young people and political (in)activism: Why don't young people vote?' *Policy & Politics*. **34** (3): 517–534; Harris, A., J. Wyn and S. Younes (2010). 'Beyond apathetic or activist youth'. *Young*. **18** (1): 9–32.

49. Berents, H. (2014). 'Slackers or delinquents? No, just politically engaged'. *The Conversation*. Online 4 June 2014.

50. Arvanitakis, J. and S. Marren (2009). *Putting the politics back into Politics: Young people and democracy in Australia.* Sydney: Whitlam Institute Discussion Paper.

51. Nasrallah, J. (2009). 'Voter turnout in Canada and Denmark'. *Canadian Parliamentary Review.* Summer: 33–37.

52. Ibid. @ 36.

53. Kimberlee, R.H. (2002). 'Why don't British young people vote at general elections?' *Journal of Youth Studies*. **5** (1): 85–98. @ 92.

54. Stoker, G. (2006). 'Explaining political disenchantment: Finding pathways to democratic renewal'. *The Political Quarterly*. **77** (2): 184–194. @ 188.

55. Kimberlee, R.H. (2002). 'Why don't British young people vote at general elections?' *Journal of Youth Studies*. **5** (1): 85–98. @ 91.

56. Ibid.

57. Harris, A., J. Wyn and S. Younes (2010). 'Beyond apathetic or activist youth'. *Young*. **18** (1): 9–32.

58. Harris, A. and J. Wyn (2009). 'Young people's politics and the micro-territories of the local'. *Australian Journal of Political Science*. **44** (2): 327–344. @ 336.

59. Henn, M., M. Weinstein and S. Forrest. (2005). 'Uninterested youth? Young people's attitudes towards party politics in Britain'. *Political Studies*. **53** (3): 556–578.

60. Ibid.

61. Harris, A., J. Wyn and S. Younes (2010). 'Beyond apathetic or activist youth'. *Young*. **18** (1): 9–32.

62. Farthing, R. (2010). 'The politics of youth antipolitics: representing the "issue" of youth participation in politics'. *Journal of Youth Studies*. **13** (2): 181–195.

63. Li, Y. and D. Marsh (2008). 'New forms of political participation: Searching for expert citizens and everyday makers'. *British Journal of Political Science*. **38** (2): 247–272. @ 250.

64. Farthing, R. (2010). 'The politics of youth antipolitics: representing the "issue" of youth participation in politics'. *Journal of Youth Studies*. **13** (2): 181–195.

65. Ibid. @ 188.

66. Ibid. @ 189.

67. Ibid. @ 190.

68. Bowman, B. (2015). 'Hate the players, love the game: why young people aren't voting'. *The Conversation*. Online 30 April 2015.

69. O'Toole, T., M. Lister, D. Marsh, S. Jones, and A. McDonagh (2003). 'Tuning out or left out? Participation and non-participation among young people'. *Contemporary Politics*. **9** (1): 45–61. @ 53.

70. Bessant, J. (2004). 'Mixed messages: Youth participation and democratic practice'. *Australian Journal of Political Science*. **39** (2): 387–404.

71. Harris, A., J. Wyn and S. Younes (2010). 'Beyond apathetic or activist youth'. *Young*. **18** (1): 9–32. @ 19.

72. Harris, A. and J. Wyn (2009). 'Young people's politics and the micro-territories of the local'. *Australian Journal of Political Science*. **44** (2): 327–344. @ 336.

73. Smith, L. and S. Thompson (2015). 'Tuning out or tuned out? A critical discourse analysis of youth political participation in Britain'. *Journal of Promotional Communications*. **3** (2): 295–301. @ 300.

74. Galston, W. A. (2007). 'Civic knowledge, civic education, and civic engagement: A summary of recent research'. *International Journal of Public Administration*. **30** (6–7): 623–642.

75. Howard, C. and S. Patten (2006). 'Valuing civics: Political commitment and the new citizenship education in Australia'. *Canadian Journal of Education*. **29** (2): 454–475. @ 455.

76. Torney-Purta, J. (2002). 'The school's role in developing civic engagement: A study of adolescents in twenty-eight Countries'. *Applied Developmental Science*. **6** (4): 203–212. @ 203.

77. Chin, K. and C. Barber (2010). 'A multi-dimensional exploration of teachers' beliefs about civic education in Australia, England, and the United States'. *Theory & Research in Social Education*. **38** (3): 395–427. @ 395.

78. Dudley, R.L. and A.R. Gitelson (2002). 'Political literacy, civic education, and civic engagement: A return to political socialization?' *Applied Developmental Science*. **6** (4): 175–182. @ 175.

79. Ross, E.W. (2004). 'Negotiating the politics of citizenship education'. *PS: Political Science and Politics*. **37** (2): 249–251. @ 249.

80. Westheimer, J. and J. Kahne (2004). 'What kind of citizen? The politics of educating for democracy'. *American Educational Research Journal*. **41** (2): 237–269. @ 237–238.

81. Howard, C. and S. Patten (2006). 'Valuing civics: Political commitment and the new citizenship education in Australia'. *Canadian Journal of Education*. **29** (2): 454–475. @ 455.

82. Farthing, R. (2012). 'Why youth participation? Some justifications and critiques of youth participation using new Labour's youth policies as a case study'. *Youth & Policy*. **109**: 71–97. @ 79.

83. Farthing, R. (2010). 'The politics of youth antipolitics: representing the "issue" of youth participation in politics'. *Journal of Youth Studies*. **13** (2): 181–195. @ 192.

REFERENCES

Arvanitakis, J. and S. Marren (2009). *Putting the politics back into politics: Young people and democracy in Australia*. Sydney, Whitlam Institute Discussion Paper.

Bastedo, H. (2015). 'Not "one of us": Understanding how non-engaged youth feel about politics and political leadership'. *Journal of Youth Studies*. **18** (5): 649–665.

Bennett, S. E. (1997). 'Why young Americans hate politics and what we should do about it'. *PS: Political Science and Politics* **30** (1): 47–53.

Berents, H. (2014). 'Slackers or delinquents? No, just politically engaged'. *The Conversation*. Online 4 June 2014.

Berg, C. (2012). 'Politics of contradiction mean democracy for me, but not for thee'. *Sydney Morning Herald*. Online 10 June 2012.

Bessant, J. (2004). 'Mixed messages: Youth participation and democratic practice'. *Australian Journal of Political Science*. **39** (2): 387–404.

Bowman, B. (2015). 'Mhairi Black goes viral: How Britain's youngest MP became a political star'. *The Conversation*. Online. 16 July 2015.

Bowman, B. (2015). 'Hate the players, love the game: Why young people aren't voting'. *The Conversation*. Online 30 April 2015.

Callick, R. and S. Gosper (2015). 'What's democracy done for me lately, asks Gen Y'. *The Australian*. Online 5 June 2012.

Chin, K. and C. Barber (2010). 'A multi-dimensional exploration of teachers' beliefs about civic education in Australia, England, and the United States'. *Theory and Research in Social Education*. **38** (3): 395–427.

Chou, M., C. Hartung and J.-P. Gagnon (2015). 'Shoten's plan to lower the voting age could help increase political engagement'. *The Conversation*. Online 2 November 2015.

Cramb, A. (2015). 'Meet Mhairi Black, Britain's youngest MP for 350 years, and an SNP firebrand'. *The Telegraph*. Online 8 May 2015.

Dalton, R. J. (2008). 'Citizenship norms and the expansion of political participation'. *Political Studies*. **56** (1): 76–98.

Dudley, R.L. and A.R. Gitelson (2002). 'Political literacy, civic education, and civic engagement: A return to political socialization?' *Applied Developmental Science*. **6** (4): 175–182.

Ercan S. A. and J.-P. Gagnon. (2014). 'The crisis of democracy: Which crisis? Which democracy?' *Democratic Theory* **1** (2): 1–10.

Evans, G. (2015). 'Play fair with young people, George Osbourne: Let 16-year-olds vote'. *The Guardian*. Online 22 July 2015.

Farthing, R. (2010). 'The politics of youth antipolitics: Representing the "issue" of youth participation in politics'. *Journal of Youth Studies* **13** (2): 181–195.

Farthing, R. (2012). 'Why youth participation? Some justifications and critiques of youth participation using new Labour's youth policies as a case study'. *Youth & Policy*. **109**: 71–97.

Farthing, R. and A. Hudson (2015). 'What would make young people get interested in politics?' *New Statesmen*. Online 9 April 2015.

Flinders, M. (2012). *Defending politics: Why democracy matters in the twenty-first century.* Oxford: Oxford University Press.

Galston, W. A. (2007). 'Civic knowledge, civic education, and civic engagement: A summary of recent research'. *International Journal of Public Administration*. **30** (6–7): 623–642.

Hanson, F. (2012). *The Lowy Institute Poll 2012: Australia and New Zealand in the world.* Sydney: Lowy Institute for International Policy.

Harris, A. and J. Wyn (2009). 'Young people's politics and the micro-territories of the local'. *Australian Journal of Political Science*. **44** (2): 327–344.

Harris, A., J. Wyn and S. Younes (2010). 'Beyond apathetic or activist youth'. *Young*. **18** (1): 9–32.

Henn, M. and N Foard (2014). 'Social Differentiation in young people's political participation: The impact of social and educational factors on youth political engagement in Britain'. *Journal of Youth Studies*. **17** (3): 360–380.

Henn, M. and M. Weinstein (2006). 'Young people and political (in)activism: Why don't young people vote?' *Policy & Politics*. **34** (3): 517–534.

Henn, M., M. Weinstein and S. Forrest. (2005). 'Uninterested youth? Young people's attitudes towards party politics in Britain'. *Political Studies* **53** (3): 556–578.

Herscovitch, B. (2012). 'Why democracy is a victim of its own success'. *Canberra Times*. Online 28 June 2012.

Howard, C. and S. Patten (2006). 'Valuing civics: Political commitment and the new citizenship education in Australia'. *Canadian Journal of Education*. **29** (2): 454–475.

Ipsos MORI. (2015). 'Political and social trends'. Online 15 December 2015.

Kimberlee, R.H. (2002). 'Why don't British young people vote at general elections?' *Journal of Youth Studies*. **5** (1): 85–98.

Li, Y. and D. Marsh (2008). 'New forms of political participation: Searching for expert citizens and everyday makers'. *British Journal of Political Science*. **38** (2): 247–272.

Martin, A. (2012). 'Political participation among the young in Australia: Testing Dalton's Good Citizen Thesis'. *Australian Journal of Political Science*. **47** (2): 211–226.

McCaffrie, B. and S. Akram (2014). 'Crisis of democracy? Recognizing the democratic potential of alternative forms of political participation'. *Democratic Theory* **1** (2): 47–55.

Nasrallah, J. (2009). 'Voter turnout in Canada and Denmark'. *Canadian Parliamentary Review*. Summer: 33–37.

Niemi, R. G. and J. D. Klingler (2012). 'The development of political attitudes and behaviour among young adults'. *Australian Journal of Political Science* **47** (1): 31–54.

Oliver, A. (2015). *The Lowy Institute Poll 2015.* Sydney, Lowy Institute for International Policy.

O'Toole, T., M. Lister, D. Marsh, S. Jones, and A. McDonagh (2003). 'Tuning out or left out? Participation and non-participation among young people'. *Contemporary Politics*. **9** (1): 45–61.

Phelps, E. (2012). 'Understanding electoral turnout among British young people: A review of the literature'. *Parliamentary Affairs*. **65** (1): 281–299.

Print, M. and L. Saha (2007). 'Youth, democracy and politics: Issues in Australia'. in Saha, L., M. Print and K. Edwards (eds.). *Youth and political participation*. Rotterdam: Sense Publishers.

Qualifications and Curriculum Authority (1998). *Education for citizenship and the teaching of democracy in schools: Final report of the Advisory Group on Citizenship (Crick Report)*. London: QCA.

Quintelier, E. (2007). 'Differences in political participation between young and old people'. *Contemporary Politics.* 13 (2): 165–180.

Ross, E.W. (2004). 'Negotiating the politics of citizenship education'. *PS: Political Science and Politics*. **37** (2): 249–251.

Runciman, D. (2013). *The confidence trap: A history of democracy in crisis from World War I to the present.* Princeton: Princeton University Press.

Russell, R. (2012). 'The surprising trends that suggest young people won't vote in 2012'. *New Republic*. Online 15 February 2012.

Sloam, J. (2015). 'How did young people vote in 2015, and what does it mean for the future?' *The Conversation*. Online 15 May 2015.

Smith, L. and S. Thompson (2015). 'Tuning out or tuned out? A critical discourse analysis of youth political participation in Britain'. *Journal of Promotional Communications* **3** (2): 295–301.

Stoker, G. (2006). 'Explaining political disenchantment: Finding pathways to democratic renewal'. *The Political Quarterly*. **77** (2): 184–194.

Tormey, S. (2015). *The end of representative politics.* Cambridge: Polity Press.

Tormey, S. (2014). 'The contemporary crisis of representative democracy'. *Democratic Theory* **1** (2): 104–112.

Torney-Purta, J. (2002). 'The school's role in developing civic engagement: A study of adolescents in twenty-eight countries'. *Applied Developmental Science*. **6** (4): 203–212.

Westheimer, J. and J. Kahne (2004). 'What kind of citizen? The politics of educating for democracy'. *American Educational Research Journal*. **41** (2): 237–269.

'Why young people don't vote'. *The Economist*. Online 29 October 2014.

'Youth Voting'. (2013). *All together now: Collaboration and innovation for youth engagement: The Report of the Commission on Youth Voting and Civic Knowledge.* Medford, Center for Information and Research on Civic Learning and Engagement.

Zeglovits, E. and J. Aichholzer (2014). 'Are people more inclined to vote at 16 than at 18? Evidence for first-time voting boost among 16- to 25-year-olds in Austria'. *Journal of Elections, Public Opinion and Parties*. **24** (3): 351–361.

Chapter Two

Democracy in Crisis

Are Young People to Blame?

Jean-Paul Gagnon

As we stated in the previous chapter, Anglo-American democracies like the United States, the United Kingdom and Australia demonstrate concern about young people's disengagement from politics. The act of not registering to vote and not voting,[1] not taking interest in parliament,[2] holding cynical opinions about politics[3] if not hating politics,[4] thoughts about how a democratic form of government may not be as good as older generations or authority figures are making it out to be[5] are all empirically observed among youth demographics in these three countries. As the American political scientist Stephen Bennett points out, there is good reason for concern here. 'Today's youth' are, after all, democracy's future. And, if today's youth 'are not prepared to assume the mantle of adult citizenship', Bennett argues, 'the future of [democracy] is bleak'.[6]

It is this empirical evidence that has led to the claim that young people today are disengaging or are already disengaged from politics. This, by extension, forms the concern that they are likely to be 'useless citizens'[7] who do not participate in public affairs and leave the running of their state to the few.[8] This is the crisis of democracy for which the young in these three Anglo-American democracies have been blamed. It is little wonder then that an education in civics is seen by certain authority figures who are concerned about young people's political disengagement as a way to nip this crisis in the bud.[9]

Yet, the narrative that '(1) young people are disengaging or disengaged from politics and are (2) thus initiating a crisis of democracy and that (3) this negative phenomenon can be arrested and reversed through civics education' is riddled with logical inconsistencies. Let's break that narrative down to further explain what we mean here.

First, and as flagged in the previous chapter, it is not the case that young people are disengaging or that they have already disengaged from politics.

Although there may be some young people who are completely apathetic about the political world around them and would consciously reject the label of being political in their apathy or of having anything to do with any manifestation of politics (should that even be possible), there are many other young people who are actively political in their own diverse ways. This much is already clear in this book, so we won't labour the point. Second, the claim that young people are initiating or have already initiated the crisis of democracy is too simplistic and does not reflect the many intricacies that are bundled in that sentence fragment. Indeed, there is an immensely large body of literature devoted to unravelling what is meant by 'the crisis of democracy'.[10] It is, therefore, our duty in this chapter to map out how the many different political practices found among young people has (a) led certain authorities to perceive that democracy is in crisis and (b) to offer a more nuanced explanation of what we think is happening in this space and what we feel to be more accurately at stake. This brings us to the third part of the narrative—that a civics curriculum can arrest and reverse the crisis of democracy. The explanation about democracy and crisis that we present in this chapter leads us to think about civics education in two ways. The first is that an education in civics *is* important and the second is that its purpose is not to perpetuate the dogma of certain forms of politics and citizenship (or democracy) at the expense of others. Rather, it should be a means for the young to explore their diverse modes of being political and to question these modes along with the conventional political institutions that they are confronted with. Ultimately, we come to the recognition that in civics education no one has the answers, and that it is up to society as a whole—especially *with* the young—to enquire about what it means to be a citizen, to be a democrat and to live in a democracy.

The purpose of this chapter is therefore to interrogate the second claim made about young people to show that what is meant by 'young people's political disengagement' cannot be equated to the 'crisis of democracy'—it is, in reality, not that simple.

To get to that point we first have to come to terms with what the concern is. What exactly *are* young people doing wrong in the eyes of certain authorities in these three Anglo-American democracies? After answering this, we then need to ask what is meant by the crisis the young are supposedly creating for democracy. Our analysis reveals that when certain authority figures claim young people are erring politically, they are in fact advocating several conceptions of democracy (which they may be conflating with democracy itself, but that's a separate issue) that they expect young people to conform to. We develop this argument further to show that certain young people are also advocating for their own conceptions of democracy and that these conceptions match up with what the literature refers to as 'young people's political practices'. A comparison of the 'authorities' conceptions' and 'young people's conceptions' of democracy shows that if there is a crisis it is more accurately about different but equally legitimate norms and practices of democracy that are *clashing* inside these democratic regimes. It is, therefore, not a case of democracy in crisis but rather a case of democracies clashing and the crisis, or crises, that spring from this. That is the first section of this chapter.

Although it becomes clear in the first section that democracy *itself* is not in crisis, and that the issue is about democracies clashing and the crises that come from this, there remains the question of how this all works. Explaining what we think to be happening is the purpose of this chapter's second section. This is done by drawing on French political theorist Pierre Rosanvallon's theory of 'counter-democracy'. This theory explains that there can be multiple 'forms' of democracy within a democratic regime and that these different forms of democracy check government and hold politicians to account. Most importantly, Rosanvallon says that governments can respond to the crises that result from one form of democracy countering another. We pick up this positive outlook on democracies countering each other, or clashing, within the regime as we feel it offers governments exciting policy opportunities.

The third section of this chapter explores where crisis fits into the clash of democracies. We find that crisis goes both ways. From the gaze of certain authority figures, political institutions deemed critical for the sustenance of democracy, like voting, appear threatened by a generation of young people who seem reluctant to take up the civic duties that authority figures expect to see in a 'good citizen'. From the gaze of certain young people, conventional political institutions seem corrupt, enthralled to big business and irrelevant to their daily lives—democracy is at risk but political reform can save it. Good citizenship is, then, about changing the system—not sustaining it. This is what we mean when we say that crisis goes both ways when democracies clash. Both camps see democracy at risk and both camps wish to save it. But in doing so, they create crises.

The fourth and final section of the chapter advances our thoughts about the synergies between conceptions of democracy and the implications this has for civics education. We come to point out that our view of civics education differs from the status quo. This is so because we align the purpose of civics education with the view that there are numerous types of democratic practices simultaneously in action within the United States, the United Kingdom and Australia and that many people including authority figures and the young are perpetuating these types of democracy. Finally, we emphasise that young people should not be perceived as naïve 'citizens-in-the-making' but rather as political agents that deserve more control over the civics education they are receiving or are to receive. Young people should be able to explore what it means to be a citizen, or a democrat living in a democracy, alongside curriculum experts, policymakers, teachers and parents.

WHAT ARE YOUNG PEOPLE DOING WRONG?
AND WHAT IS MEANT BY THE CRISIS
THEY ARE SUPPOSEDLY CREATING?

Young people have been predominantly accused of lacking political knowledge;[11] being cynical towards politics;[12] apathetic to duty norms;[13] non-traditional (i.e. not conforming with historical or conventional understandings of political practice);[14] distrustful of political institutions, political parties, politicians and governments;[15] less willing than their parents to join political parties;[16] disinterested in politics;[17] not enrolling to vote and not voting;[18] ignoring public authority;[19] lacking conviction in their democratic institutions;[20] and of being distracted by work.[21,22] 'The political disconnect', write Henn, Weinstein and Hodkinson, 'amongst British citizens is particularly acute amongst young people'.[23] The same has been said about young people in the United States[24] and Australia.[25]

Checkoway et al. state 'that these are the types of views that permeate the news media, social science and professional practice when referring to young people'.[26] It is certainly a long list of indictments.

The first recognition that needs to be made in the face of these indictments is that most of them are not, actually, found only among the young. For example, being distracted by work is a problem for older generations too. This resonates with the literature critical of neoliberal consumer capitalism and how this socioeconomic structure leaves little time for labourers (or the agents in the structure) to be political or to even think about politics. People, in this structure, are preoccupied with working long hours, caring for dependants, doing house work, saving to buy high-value goods, undertaking full-time study with the hope of entering a 'non-political profession' and so forth. 'Perhaps you know the joke', writes Stanley Aronowitz, 'we are born, we go to school, we get a job (either for wages or unpaid work at home), we get married and have kids (or not), and then we die'.[27] The joke, Aronowitz says, 'is about the life cycle and is meant to convey the utter banality of human existence'. What he goes onto show, however, is that if life appears banal it is because of the capitalist structure that keeps people's 'noses to the grindstone'. Hassan brings this point home by arguing that there is a 'temporal mismatch' between the neoliberal economy and democratic institutions—individuals of all ages are today caught up in the speed of production and consumption with little time to think about democracy and what it means to be a citizen in one. Much has already been written showing that many of the accusations levelled at young people about being politically disengaged are also observable in older groups. Although, as seen in the first chapter, the statistical significance is in recent years usually lower for those older groups (e.g. younger people are for instance, on average, more likely to feel alienated by politics when compared with their grandparents). This is one point that we can grasp. Young people today are *more likely* than older demographics to feel or think in ways that reflect the indictments levelled against them.

There is, however, another observation that particularly singles out the young. It is that they are breaking with tradition or convention and thus what authority figures perceive to be the 'right' way—if not the only way—of participating politically or of being a citizen. Take, for instance, the experience of the builder generation after the Second World War. The 1950s were halcyon days for electoral, party and voting democracy.[28] Builders were apparently more trusting of politicians. The large majority of them voted. Many joined political parties and attended union meetings (except in the United States, which has always had low union membership when compared with the United Kingdom and Australia). But then came the snap. Boomers emerged as youths predominantly in the 1960s and early 1970s. What many young boomers saw in this time was, to offer but a few examples, ethnic and gender discrimination, the political disenfranchisement of visible minorities, growing material inequality, corruption among politicians, proxy wars (e.g. Vietnam) and urban squalor. The political structure that these boomers found themselves in was the product of the builders' generation and the silent generation before them. Many young boomers found that this structure perpetuated racism, discrimination, damaging stereotypes about women, homophobia and more. Political parties were either unresponsive to these so-called post-materialist issues or had their hands tied by opinion polls and political advisors (e.g. it would have been 'political suicide' for a major party to come out with strong, progressive, policies to address the issues that concerned many young boomers). Thus, a significant proportion of the young engaged in alternative forms of political participation—they protested and helped give rise to the Civil Rights movement. For some authorities, this was a case of 'too much democracy' and 'participatory overload'—both of which were causing a crisis of democracy.[29] The feeling in the mid-1970s was that young people were misbehaving and that they should return to practicing politics 'correctly'—meaning that they should join political parties, vote and petition authority figures as their parents and grandparents may have done. Taken together, the issue is that young people demonstrate on average a higher level of disengagement than older generations from *conventional* politics. This is where the young have gone wrong in the eyes of certain authority figures.

What we, at this point, need to ascertain is how this issue translates into a crisis of democracy. What, exactly, is meant by 'crisis' and 'democracy' here?

The answer to the question of crisis is fairly straightforward. Young people's political behaviour is different from that of their parents and grandparents. This worries authority figures as, in their eyes, the political practices of older generations is what sustained and continues to sustain democracy.

That young people are not, for example, voting, staying abreast of political events and actors and so on, is therefore a sign of crisis because young people *are* the future of democracy. Once they 'grow up', if they can't explain the purpose of the legislative, executive and judicial functions of government, or tell the difference between a democracy and an oligarchy, or bother to voice their opinions on ballot papers, what hope is there? From this perspective, it is clear that this is a crisis that needs to be addressed through a policy of more or better civic education and that this should be provided to young people as part of their compulsory schooling.

The answer to the question over democracy is less obvious. That a statistically significant proportion of young people are disengaging or are already disengaged from conventional political practices is causing a crisis of democracy presupposes that certain authority figures understand what democracy is in the first place. This is logically problematic as democracy is 'an essentially contested concept'.[30] There are, for example, more than 1,200 different ways of describing the word 'democracy' and potentially as many ways of practicing it, seeing it practiced or thinking about how it should be practiced.[31] Faced with the reality that democracy can mean different things to different people, it behoves us then to try to identify *which* democracy young people are allegedly putting into crisis.

One way of ascertaining this is by examining 'American democracy', 'British democracy' and 'Australian democracy'. The trouble though is that each of these three conceptions of democracy are also sites of ontological contestation. If one thing is true about each of these conceptions it is that they are the product of *many* democracies in action *at* the same time *and* over time. Take American democracy as one example (it is potentially the most widely used conception of democracy in English scholarly literature by a wide margin).[32] In the early 1800s, when Tocqueville and Beaumont were travelling in the United States they found themselves caught in a period of contestation over the meaning of democracy. The political historian Lee Benson describes how the volatility of political factions—these tumultuous starting points for the Democratic and Republican parties—stirred confusion over what democracy in America was supposed to mean. Here we see epithets like Hamiltonian democracy, Jeffersonian democracy, Jacksonian democracy and Van Buren democracy, in use. Their proponents used these epithets to contest whether American democracy should be popular and populist or restrained, in the republican sense, by a wealthy or otherwise meritocratic elite (or, imaginably, even some mix of the two).[33] The confusion over American democracy does not end there. Leo Damrosch, in his retelling of Tocqueville and Beaumont's travels, shows that they also came across altogether different concepts of democracy both on the East coast and at the frontier, in Ohio.[34] On the East coast, one of the first impressions they formed of American democracy was that it was mercantilist, business-oriented and materially focused.[35] At the frontier, Tocqueville and Beaumont experienced 'unalloyed democracy':[36] Ohio, at the time, was 'a society that as yet has no bonds, political, hierarchical, social, religious . . . [it was] a democracy without limit or moderation'. Or, as Frederick Jackson Turner once wrote, 'American democracy was born of no theorists' dream; it was not carried in the Susan Constant to Virginia, nor in the Mayflower to Plymouth. It came stark and strong and full of life out of the American forest, and it gained new strength each time it touched a new frontier'.[37] Damrosch captures the struggle over American democracy well in his retelling of some advice that Francis Lieber gave to Tocqueville: 'democracy' he said is 'as much a state of mind as a political system'.[38] Fast forwarding to today, it seems that the contestation over what American democracy is or is not has only become more multi-chorused and remains equally inchoate.[39] Similar arguments can be made for both British and Australian democracy.

So, trying to ascertain what certain authorities in these Anglo-American democracies mean by democracy by looking at the country-oriented literature is not much help. What this recognition does achieve, however, is to show that if an authority figure claims that a young person is putting American, British or Australian democracy at risk by, say, not voting, it is clear that such a claim does not reflect the long-standing and undeniable pluralism underlying these conceptions of democracy.

A different way of ascertaining what certain authorities mean by democracy is to transform their indictments levelled at young people into positive claims and to then ask which conceptions of democracy these claims match up with in the literature. Table 2.1 shows the schematic. The young are meant to be politically knowledgeable, trusting towards political institutions, political parties, politicians and governments; actively upholding civic duties; and holding conventional understandings of political practice. They are supposed to be more willing to join political parties; to be interested in politics; enrolled to vote and voting; obey public authority; have conviction in their democratic institutions; and not be distracted by work. The method used to match political expectation with conception of democracy is fairly straightforward. Does, for example, the need to be politically knowledgeable appear as a normative claim in one, or more, conceptions of democracy? If yes, which one(s)? It is important to flag that table 2.1 is not self-evident or axiomatically 'true'. It is, simply, an example to show that when certain authorities say 'democracy' they are, in fact, speaking of 'democracies'. In other words, if you were to use this method yourself, and search the literature for which conception of democracy holds having political knowledge as one of its normative claims, you might end up with a conception different to Deweyan democracy (which is the conception we ended up with). This, of course, would be completely fine for us as here we are not setting out to say that 'political knowledge' matches best, or only, with 'Deweyan democracy'. Rather, we are only trying to show that certain authority figures are referring to multiple conceptions of democracy in the claims they are making about young people's political disengagement.

What Table 2.1 reveals is that certain authority figures advocate numerous conceptions of democracy. This flips the logic of the crisis of democracy on its head because what is now meant is that young people's political disengagement puts *democracies* into crisis. But this view is only true if one believes that young people are not participating in politics when they disengage with the many democracies identified in the table below.

The key here is to recognise that authorities mean different conceptions of democracy when they write or utter that word. The point is not to count all of the possibilities or to haggle over methods of aligning what an authority figure says and how that ends up championing a specific type of democracy. That's for a different work altogether. All that we can say is that authority figures are advancing numerous conceptions of democracy that seem to be clustering around voting, being knowledgeable about politics, trusting your representatives and government, obeying public authority and believing in the conventional or historical *mores* of democracy in one's country.

Now for the twist. If certain authority figures advance conceptions of democracy through their criticism of young people, it is probable that those same young people will be advancing *their own* conceptions of democracy

Table 2.1   **Matching Authorities' Political Expectations with Conceptions of Democracy**

Political expectation		*Conception(s) of democracy*
1. Be politically knowledgeable	→	Deweyan democracy[40]
2. Trust (have faith) in political institutions, political parties, politicians and governments	→	Modern democracy[41]
3. Uphold civic duty norms	→	Voting democracy[42]
4. Have conventional understandings of political practice	→	Traditional democracy and historical democracy[43]
5. Willingness to join political parties	→	Representative democracy[44]
6. Interest in politics	→	Voting democracy[45]
7. Registered to vote and voting	→	Voting democracy, electoral democracy,[46] representative democracy
8. Obey public authority	→	Republican democracy[47]
9. Have conviction (believe) in democratic institutions	→	Cultural democracy[48]
10. Not be distracted by work	→	Liberal democracy[49]

too. As Pippa Norris writes, 'the older focus on citizenship activities designed to influence elections, government, and public policy-making process within the nation-state, seems unduly limited today, by excluding too much that is commonly understood as broadly "political"'.[50] Young people, as major bodies of literature show, *are* politically active. They are politically active on the Internet[51] and through social media;[52] their politics is cause-oriented[53] and post-materialist.[54] Many young people are radically unpolitical[55] and more likely to participate in the informal politics of collecting signatures[56] for or 'signing petitions, [collecting or] donating money to campaigns, joining campaign groups, and participating in demonstrations'.[57] They take part in 'localised social action activities', which includes 'volunteering, informal community networks, informal political action, awareness-raising, altruistic acts, and general campaigning'[58] but are also involved in 'big national and/ or global political issues'.[59] In short, certain young people seem to be doing all kinds of politics outside of the authorities' expectations. There is a greater tendency here to disobey public authority—especially in the realm of demonstration and protest. Matters get messy, however, when it comes to *mores* because all of these different 'young person's' political activities are not unconventional if we take the last sixty years of political history in the United States, the United Kingdom and Australia into account. Nor are they culturally alien to Anglo-American democracies. So what gives?

Table 2.2 is revealing here. As with table 2.1, it matches what young people *are* said to be doing politically as opposed to what certain authorities feel they *should* be doing, with conceptions of democracy. The contrast between both sets of conceptions is telling. We can observe, for instance, how the conceptions of democracy associated with certain young people's political practices

Table 2.2   Matching Young People's Political Practices with Wonceptions of Democracy

Political practice		Conception(s) of democracy
1. Online	→	E-democracy,[61] electronic democracy,[62] digital democracy[63]
2. Through social media	→	Social media democracy,[64] Facebook democracy[65]
3. Cause-oriented	→	Advocacy democracy[66]
4. Post-materialist	→	Green democracy[67]
5. Radical and civilly disobedient	→	Radical democracy,[68] direct democracy[69]
6. Unpolitical	→	Unpolitical democracy[70]
7. Informal	→	Informal democracy[71]
8. Local	→	Alternative democracy[72]
9. Global	→	Cosmopolitan democracy[73]
10. Social, community-oriented	→	Decentralised democracy[74]

coalesces around spaces outside of formal arena politics and conventional political institutions. The emphasis is on post-material and issue-specific politics—such as environmental concerns which often bridge both local and global politics—that are social and community oriented. So, although certain young people do feel displeasure with formal, traditional, conventional and so forth, types of politics, the second section of this chapter shows—yet again—that many young people are not disengaged. They are only 'doing politics differently'.[60]

What this comparative analysis leaves us with is the understanding that certain authority figures and certain young people are promoting different conceptions of democracy through the ways in which they practise or understand politics. Table 2.1 emphasises conventional political practices like voting, elections and representation. Table 2.2 emphasises other political practices like not voting, protesting specific legislation online or in the streets and trying to effect political change through local–global associations. The issue is, therefore, not a case of young people causing a crisis of democracy, but rather that crises are produced by democracies clashing. This is a different take on the crisis of democracy narrative found in the civics education debate. Let's now take a closer look at what it means when democracies clash by first examining *how* they clash.

HOW DEMOCRACIES CLASH

Pierre Rosanvallon's theory of 'counter-democracy' helps to explain the clash of democracies happening in the United States, the United Kingdom and Australia. 'Rosanvallon', writes Gareth Stedman Jones, 'believes that conventional definitions of democracy, which restrict it to the electoral process, are too narrow. A more adequate account would include the various ways in which the people are able to check or hold to account their representatives or the government, irrespective of electoral process'.[75] Although Rosanvallon does not go as far as we do in acknowledging the plurality of conceptions of democracy that 'check' or 'hold' politicians and/or governments, he makes an important point about democracy's 'forms' which applies equally well in the context of this chapter. Different 'forms' of democracy, he says, act against each other in democratic regimes. Rosanvallon sees one form of democracy countering another form of democracy as a balancing act between competing democratic practices and democratic values *within* a democratic regime. The nature of this competition, including the forms of democracy that clash with one another, changes over time depending on who is alive, when, doing and thinking what, and in which social, economic, political and cultural contexts, with which technologies and communicative media they have available to them, and so forth. Rosanvallon sees this competition as inherently good. It can keep a democratic regime relevant to its times because such a regime should reflect people's conceptions of democracy and express the crises that occur when democracies clash within it. This may even fulfil John Dewey's condition that democratic regimes should always be reinventing themselves so that they stay up to date and resonant with the people that live within them.[76] Dewey, as Kathy Hytten writes, 'reminds us of the importance of context, maintaining that democracy must emerge from the concerns, values, habits and practices of cultural groups. It is never something that can be imposed from above or achieved through undemocratic means'. To quote Dewey directly:

> [T]he very idea of democracy, the meaning of democracy, must continually be explored afresh; it has to be constantly discovered, and rediscovered, remade and reorganized; while the political and economic and social institutions in which it is embodied have to [continuously] be remade and reorganized.[77]

The clash of democracies is such a process of renewal as each conception of democracy advances its own normative claim and potentially even political practice. It is these norms and practices that people, 'young and old', breathe life into through their conviction that one conception of democracy (which most people probably conflate with democracy itself) is or may be more legitimate than another. 'Green democracy' could, for example, be more legitimate than 'electoral democracy' in the eyes of a young person because it deals directly with a spectrum of environmental concerns that major political parties seem unable, or unwilling, to address. That's the norm: then comes the practice. A young person who feels this way might take the next step and support international political agitations for more and better policy responses to environmental degradation by signing a petition online, sharing 'green manifestos' on social networking sites like Facebook or Twitter, or even entering a competition to win free travel to a multinational concert promoting action against climate change. They may even connect with local, community-level, environmental programmes or protests. The reverse is just as apt an example. An authority figure, such as a politician, may consistently receive quality scientific evidence showing that young people are—by a significant statistical margin—less knowledgeable about politics and democracy than older generations or a similar cohort of young people in other countries. This, along with the petitions that the politician might receive from parents, teachers and civics experts, and the media reports commenting on the same evidence the politician was given, could prompt her to see Deweyan democracy as valuable—if not essential—to the welfare of democracy. As Dewey's conception of democracy emphasises the importance of political knowledge[78] (something he views as a core requirement for citizens to keep their democracy in good health), the politician would not be wrong in seeing the practice of more or better non-partisan education in politics (i.e. civics) as a legitimate policy response to a perceived crisis of democracy. Both positions reflect the legitimate politics of specific people within a democratic regime and both advance norms and practices that are arguably of equal importance for sustaining a democratic regime.

This is how democracies clash. There could be dozens, possibly even hundreds, of clashes happening concurrently within countries like the United States, the United Kingdom and Australia due to the many different conceptions of democracy that individuals, or groups of people, advocate in their professional or everyday political beliefs and practices. Explanatory power here rests with the reasons that drive individuals or groups to advocate for one or more conceptions of democracy. For some young people, these reasons include alienation from formal arena politics, dissatisfaction with major political parties or electoral systems, cynicism about politicians' broken promises and the irrelevance of politicians as many are, or appear to be, disinterested in the policy concerns commonly found among the young. A young person may see conventional politics as a place with little to no traction for them. So they focus elsewhere: on informal, online, alternative and radical politics that clash with conventional politics because they require norms and practices that differ from those found in the mainstream.

THE CRISES (AND OPPORTUNITIES) IN THE CLASH

In reading Rosanvallon's book *Counter-Democracy: Politics in an Age of Distrust* (masterfully translated by Arthur Goldhammer), we were drawn to a line he used in the introduction: that he was going to examine political distrust in democracies by looking specifically at how 'different societies have *responded* to the dysfunctions of representative regimes'[79] (emphasis added). It is, specifically, this idea of response on the part of society that captured our attention. The clash of democracies produces crises that differ in duration (acute versus diffuse), degree (mild, moderate, severe, fatal), location (e.g. level of government or political institution) and category (e.g. legitimation, function and tradition).[80] Rosanvallon's emphasis on response led us to view the crises that emanate from the clash of democracies as events that can be responded to by both authority figures and young people.[81]

One way of understanding this idea of an opportunity within a crisis is to break down the crisis into its qualifiers (i.e. duration, degree, location and category) and to then theorise which opportunities come out of each qualifier. The following example shows what we mean here. If young people were experiencing a crisis of e-democracy, perhaps because of actions that a government is taking to strengthen face-to-face political practices in a bid to return to more conventional political practices (i.e. traditional democracy), young people would do well to enquire into the nature of this crisis emanating from the clash between e-democracy and traditional democracy. The young people concerned might, for instance, see that this is an acute crisis because e-democracy has been growing—and will likely continue to grow—in popularity.[82] If a government is combating this trend it may be doing so because of its conservative and security values. An appropriate, if not productive, response to this crisis could therefore be for young people to start a values-based, pro e-democracy campaign through social media to counter or appease these conservative and security values.

Crisis, it should be noted, goes both ways depending on whose gaze we are viewing the crisis from. Voting democracy, for example, is commonly considered to be in crisis especially in the United States and the United Kingdom—two democratic regimes without compulsory voting. The longitudinal trend seems to indicate that fewer and fewer young people are bothering to register as voters and to turn up to vote for national, state and local elections.[83] In Australia, which has compulsory voting, registering to vote and casting ballots is not as much of a concern as it is in the United States and the United Kingdom. However, a recent study suggests that spoiling ballot papers is more common among young Australian voters than it is among older generations.[84] Why is this the case? One answer is that radical democracy—or the legitimate practice of being civilly disobedient by for instance practicing abstention from being a voter and voting—holds strong normative appeal for many young people. By *not* voting they are challenging the value of the vote, rebuking the authority-imposed civic duty of voting and showing that there is one or more problems—like a lack of proportionality, and therefore mathematical fairness, in the election of national legislative assemblies in the United States, the United Kingdom and Australia. Our reading of Rosanvallon suggests that the appropriate response by governments and other authority figures, who prize voting democracy, would be to treat this crisis emanating from the clash between voting and radical democracy as an opportunity. This is fundamentally different to the approach taken to date in civics curricula which do not explore the crisis of voting *with* young people but rather seek to convince them of how important voting is and how dangerous[85] it is for their democratic regime if one does not express their political voice, through a ballot paper, when it is due.

Table 2.3 lays out the situation. On the left side of the table are the types of crisis (duration, degree, location and category) that emanate from the clash between radical democracy and voting democracy. Details for each type of crisis are given for the United States, the United Kingdom and Australian

Table 2.3   The Crisis of Voting Democracy and the Opportunities this Presents

Types of crisis	Anglo-American Democracy			Opportunity
	US	*UK*	*Aus*	
Crisis of duration	Acute, during elections. And diffuse, between elections.	•	•	Explore why cynicism about voting persists among young people and produce policies to mitigate the issues raised. Explore the psychology of voting: does cynicism increase among certain young people during elections? Why?
Crisis of degree	Severe	Severe	Mild	The United States and United Kingdom should see this as an emergency and take major action. Australia should study spoiled ballot papers and young dissenters for policy insights.
Crisis of location	Voter registration, voting in person, voting online, postal votes, ballot papers.	•	•	Civil servants should be incentivised to register voters; make registration easier; improve in person, postal and/or online voting services; create an app that allows the user to practice filling out different ballot papers; produce social advertisement explaining the value of the vote/ dangers of not voting.
Category of crisis	Legitimacy. The inherent value of the vote is at risk.	•	•	Explore why young people devalue the vote and enact policies to help bring value back into ballot papers.

contexts. This is followed, on the right hand side of the table, by the policy opportunities that governments in these democratic regimes can, and should, take in response to these crises. The table views the clash from the perspective of voting democracy on the defensive (i.e. that radical democracy is creating a crisis for voting democracy).

The point here is to show that crisis goes both ways when democracies clash. It affects young people and authority figures but also presents opportunities for both parties when a particular crisis—like the crisis of e-democracy or voting democracy—is analytically unpacked.

It is worth highlighting that the clash of democracies is a *good* phenomenon to be seeing within democratic regimes. It shows that people (which people and how many is a different question) in the regime are diverse in their political norms and practices. It shows that when these norms and practices come into contestation with each other this creates sites of crisis that authority figures and young people can respond to. Recognising and responding to crises born out of democracies clashing—thinking particularly about Dewey's views on the need for democratic regimes to continuously reinvent themselves—is a necessary condition for a healthy democratic regime. It helps to keep the regime resilient, nimble and relevant in that 'up-with-the-times' kind of way.

Counter-democracy can, to some people, come across as counter-intuitive. How, for instance, can a clash between two different conceptions of democracy be anything but a negative and the sign of a broken society? The answer lies in how agents approach the crises produced by these clashes. The status quo approach in Anglo-American democracies has been unreflective. There is a taken-for-granted a priori knowledge of democracy by certain authorities *and* certain young people. The ontological difficulties inherent to democracy are not worked through in the way that we have done in this chapter. And so, in the mainstream, we get these logically flawed claims like the one we began this chapter with: that young people are disengaging or are already disengaged from politics, that this is causing a crisis of democracy and that this crisis must be arrested and reversed through civics education. A different approach is to view certain young people as disengaging or disengaged from particular political norms and practices, but that many young people are advocating for their own conceptions of democracy. These democracies clash with the conceptions of democracy that certain authority figures have been advocating; these clashes create numerous sites of crisis, and there are opportunities in these crises. All of this points to a need to fundamentally rethink the purpose of civics education.

IMPLICATIONS FOR CIVICS EDUCATION

We end this chapter with a discussion on the opportunities that could be nurtured between clashing conceptions of democracy and what this implies for civics education. Let's return to the example of a young person's green democracy and a politician's Deweyan democracy. The young person, presumably, may have no or little interest in the formal political schooling the politician is advocating, much as the politician may have little to no interest in the local environmental programme the young person is advocating. Both agents' means and ends do not align and it becomes a crisis of legitimation for them: 'if the young person is indifferent to civics education' or if 'the politician does not care for my community's environmental program' then what good is that young person or that politician for my understanding of democracy, for my ideal society or for me and my immediate concerns?

The way out of this legitimation crisis, which we are indebted to Rosanvallon for establishing, is for authorities and young people to look for synergies between their conceptions of democracy. Clashes need not be divisive or irreconcilable—although some of them will be—and there is good in that too as the theory of agonistic democracy does so well to explain.[86] One potential policy solution to the green democracy—Deweyan democracy clash would be for the politician to ask her policy community to come up with a strategy for integrating local environmental programmes and global environmental movements that are accessible online into schools' civics curricula. Although our young person here may scoff at this, seeing it as yet another instance of authority trying to 'trick' subordinates into engaging with conventional politics by co-opting the green issue, it may nevertheless legitimately win over the hearts of other, less opposed, young people and increase the chances of sustaining *both* green and Deweyan conceptions of democracy. And although a similar argument can be made for this young person to try to find how a formal civics education can help her upskill in politics or increase the chances of her community's environmental campaign succeeding, we must recognise that she is in the disadvantaged position here. The politician's power is formidable when compared to the young person's. The obligation then, to look for synergies between conceptions of democracy, should fall principally on the politician, on governments and on other authority figures because it is they who have the most power to come up with responsible policy solutions to the crises that come about when democracies clash. Further to this, if authority figures see that many young people are suspicious of their solutions, it is their responsibility to open dialogue with young people to explore this. The same can be said in the obverse: if young people see that authority figures are suspicious of *their* solutions then these young people should try to explore why that is the case.

This idea of looking for synergies between different conceptions of democracy has implications for the way we understand civics education. Normatively, civics education should try to engage with as many conceptions and practices of democracy as possible. Young people, teachers and parents should have the opportunity to critique different conceptions, to explore their normative imperatives and to weigh one against another. This could create a fruitful environment of enquiry within the school where authority figures and young people can debate the promises and problems inherent in their contrasting conceptions of democracy. Part of this enquiry could be to look for the value in synergising contrasting conceptions of democracy or in the importance of sustaining their differences. This could even lead to thinking about which policy solutions may reinvigorate existing political institutions. Examples include how deliberative democratic practices can strengthen the institutions that underpin representative democracy. Or how green democracy will always bring the focus of policymakers back to environmental concerns—even if that reminder means the policy may have to change, see its progress through parliament slow or be rejected.

Overall, in this chapter we have argued that young people are not to blame for the crisis of democracy because—with reference to political disengagement and civics education—there is in reality no one crisis to address. This is because the meaning of democracy is plural. We showed, for instance, how the claims advanced by certain authority figures about young people's disengagement are advancing numerous legitimate conceptions of democracy but that these conceptions are being countered by the numerous other legitimate conceptions of democracy that certain young people are advancing through their everyday politics. This is where crisis, or crises, is to be found. It comes out of the clash of democracies. Importantly, this is not a symptom of sick democracy, but rather a signal of a healthy democratic regime—one that is, and must remain, characterised by the crises that come from democracies countering each other within the regime and the policy solutions that authority figures, young people or society at large take in response to them. It is our view that civics education should nurture this perspective on democracy and crisis. We think this way because it shows that many young people are active political agents in their own right and that they should be given the opportunity to work alongside policymakers and civics experts. Together, they can co-produce a civics education for the future where, if anything is to blame, it would be our ignorance over the irreducibly plural, clashing world of democracies and of all the opportunities that lie within it.

NOTES

1. Kimberlee, R. H. (2010). 'Why Don't British Young People Vote at General Elections?' *Journal of Youth Studies* **5** (1): 85–98.

2. Kelso, A. (2007). 'Parliament and Political Disengagement: Neither Waving nor Drowning'. *Political Quarterly* **78** (3): 364–373. @ 8–9. Kelso explains how Westminster has been attempting to engage young people so that they receive more education about legislation before becoming voters. This, however, is framed in

Kelso's wider argument that young people (and older generations) are not visiting Westminster as often as MPs feel they should be which helps to explain why Westminster has a public outreach programme in place.

3. Quintelier, E. (2007). 'Differences in Political Participation between Young and Old People'. *Contemporary Politics* **13** (12): 165–180.

4. Bennett, S. E. (1997). 'Why Young Americans Hate Politics, and What We Should Do about It'. *PS: Political Science & Politics* **30** (1): 47–53.

5. Chou, M. (2013). 'Democracy's Not for Me: The Lowy Institute Polls on Gen Y and Democracy'. *Australian Journal of Political Science* **48** (4): 485–494.

6. Bennett, S. E. (1997). @ 50.

7. H. M. van de Bovenkamp. (2010). *'The Limits of Patient Power: Examining Active Citizenship in Dutch Health Care'*. Dissertation. Erasmus University Rotterdam. @ 12.

8. Bennett, S. E. (1997). @ 50.

9. Storrie, T. (1997). 'Citizens or What?' In Jeremy Roche, Stanley Tucker, Rachel Thomson, Ronny Flynn (Eds) *Youth in Society*. London: Sage. pp. 52–60.

10. See, for recent examples of this diverse literature: Avritzer, L. (2012). 'Democracy beyond Aggregation: The Participatory Dimension of Public Deliberation'. *Journal of Public Deliberation* **8** (2): n/a; Dahl, A., and J. Soss. (2014). 'Neoliberalism for the Common Good? Public Value Governance and the Downsizing of Democracy'. *Public Administration Review* **74** (4): 496–504; Marsh, D. (2014). 'What Is the Nature of the Crisis of Democracy and What Can We Do About It?' *Democratic Theory* **1** (2): 37–46; Nicolaïdis, K. (2013). 'European Democracy and its Crisis'. *Journal of Common Market Studies* **51** (2): 351–369; Tamura, T., and Y. H. Kobayashi. (2014). 'Niggling New Democracies in the Age of Individualization in Japan'. *Democratic Theory* **1** (2): 122–130.

11. Galston, W. A. (2004). 'Civic Education and Political Participation'. *PS: Political Science & Politics* **37** (2): 263–266. @ 263.

12. Grattan, M. (2006). *'The New Political Crisis'*. The Age 7 October.

13. Ibid.

14. Ibid.

15. Ibid.; J. Dermody, and S. Hanmerlloyd. (2005). 'Safeguarding the Future of Democracy: (Re)building Young People's Trust in Parliamentary Politics'. *Journal of Political Marketing* **4** (2–3): 115–133. @ 125. Loss of faith in government may be a recent trend, at least in the United States, as Uslaner states (in 1997) that 'trust in government . . . is the province of the young'. See E. M. Uslaner. (1997). 'Is Washington Really the Problem?' In J. R. Hibbing and E. Theiss-Morse (Eds.). *What Is It about Government that Americans Dislike?* Cambridge: Cambridge University Press. pp. 118–133. @ 123.

16. Tom, E. (2006). *'What's Australia Day to You Is Elton's Chunder to Them'*. **29** November.

17. Ibid.

18. Rubin, T. (2014). 'Democracy Loses Luster 25 Years after Berlin Wall's Fall'. *The Knoxville News Sentinel*. 16 November.

19. Author unknown. (2007). 'Jolting Gen Y to Act'. *Sunday Times* (Perth). 24 June.

20. C. W. Ruitenberg. (2009). 'Educating Political Adversaries: Chantal Mouffe and Radical Democratic Citizenship Education'. *Studies in Philosophical Education* **28** (3): 269–281. @ 279.

21. Ribarich, J. (2013). 'Should We Lower the Voting Age to 16?' *Crikey*. 5 November.

22. Sloam gives a similar list of indictments. '[D]ecreasing participation in civic life, low levels of trust in political institutions, the individualization of lifestyles, values, and risks, the depoliticization of public policy, and growing cynicism about electoral politics in the media'. See Sloam, J. (2014). 'New Voice, Less Equal: The Civic and Political Engagement of Young People in the United States and Europe'. *Comparative Political Studies* **47** (5): 663–688. @ 664.

23. Henn, M., M. Weinstein, and S. Hodgkinson. (2007). 'Social Capital and Political Participation: Understanding the Dynamics of Young People's Political Disengagement in Contemporary Britain'. *Social Policy & Society* **6** (4): 467–479. @ 468.

24. Sloam (2014) @ 664.

25. Edwards, K. (2009). 'Disenfranchised Not "Deficient": How the (Neoliberal) State Disenfranchises Young People'. *Australian Journal of Social Issues* **44** (1): 23–37. @ 24.

26. Checkoway, B., K. Richards-Schuster, S. Abdulla, M. Aragon, E. Facio, L. Figueroa, E. Reddy, M. Welsh, and A. White. (2003). 'Young People as Competent Citizens'. *Community Development Journal* **38** (4): 298–309. @ 299.

27. Aronowitz, S. (2001). *The Last Good Job in America: Work and Education in the New Global Technoculture.* Lanham: Rowman & Littlefield.

28. Greider, W. (1992). *Who Will Tell the People: The Betrayal of American Democracy.* New York: Simon & Schuster. @ 19.

29. Crozier, M., S. P. Huntington, and J. Watanuki. (1975). *The Crisis of Democracy: Report on the Governability of Democracies to the Trilateral Commission.* New York: New York University Press.

30. Doughty, Howard A. (2014). 'Democracy as an Essentially Contested Concept'. *The Innovation Journal: The Public Sector Innovation Journal* **19** (1): 1–21.

31. Gagnon, J.-P. (2016). *'Democracy's Adjective Pluralism'.* Working Paper.

32. Ibid.

33. Benson, L. (1961). *The Concept of Jacksonian Democracy: New York as a Test Case.* Princeton: Princeton University Press. @ 3–11.

34. Damrosch, L. (2010). *Tocqueville's Discovery of America.* New York: Farrar, Strauss, and Giroux.

35. Ibid. @ 25.

36. Ibid. @ 136–137.

37. Ibid. @ 69.

38. Ibid. @ 106.

39. Schlozman, K. L., S. Verba, and H. Brady. (2012). *The Unheavenly Chorus: Unequal Political Voice and the Broken Promise of American Democracy.* Princeton: Princeton University Press.

40. Comber, Melissa K. (2007). 'Political Participation and Service Learning: Civic Education as Problem and Solution'. In D. M. Shea and J. C. Green (Eds). *Fountain of Youth: Strategies and Tactics for Mobilizing America's Young Voters.* Lanham: Rowman & Littlefield.

41. Zmerli, S., K. Newton, and J. R. Montero. (2007). 'Trust in People, Confidence in Political Institutions, and Satisfaction with Democracy'. In J. W. van Deth, J. R. Montero, and Anders Westholm (Eds). *Citizenship and Involvement in European Democracies: A Comparative Analysis.* London: Routledge.

42. McCaffrie, B., and Sadiya Akram. (2014). 'Crisis of Democracy? Recognizing the Democratic Potential of Alternative Forms of Political Participation'. *Democratic Theory* **1** (2): 47–55. @ 50.

43. Gamble, A. (1990). 'Theories of British Politics'. *Political Studies* **38** (3): 404–420.

44. Dräger, J., and R. Roth. (2011). 'Adapting to Change Instead of Heading for Crisis—Challenges and Opportunities for Democracy in Germany'. In *Vitalizing Democracy Through Participation.* Gütersloh: Verlag Bertelsmann Stiftung. pp. 15–28.

45. Almond, G. A., and Sidney Verba. (1963). *The Civic Culture: Political Attitudes and Democracy in Five Nations.* Princeton: Princeton University Press.

46. Franklin, M. N., and S. B. Hobolt. (2011). 'The Legacy of Lethargy: How Elections to the European Parliament Depress Turnout'. *Electoral Studies* **30** (1): 67–76.

47. Slaughter, S. (2007). 'Cosmopolitan and Republican Citizenship'. In W. Hudson and S. Slaughter (Eds). *Globalisation and Citizenship: The Transnational Challenge.* London: Routledge. pp. 85–99.

48. Griffith, E. S., J. Plamenatz, and J. R. Pennock. (1956). 'Cultural Prerequisites to a Successfully Functioning Democracy: A Symposium'. *American Political Science Review* **50** (1): 101–137.

49. Beetham, D. (1992). 'Liberal Democracy and the Limits of Democratization'. *Political Studies* **46** (5): 40–53. @ 47.

50. Norris, P. (2004). 'Young People and Political Activism: From the Politics of Loyalties to the Politics of Choice?' Report for the Council of Europe Symposium. 'Young People and Democratic Institutions: From Disillusionment to Participation'. Strasbourg, 27–28 November. Available online: https://www.hks.harvard.edu/fs/pnorris/Acrobat/COE%20Young%20People%20and%20Political%20Activism.pdf. @ 5.

51. Bakker, T. P., and C. H. de Vreese. (2011). 'Good News for the Future? Young People, Internet Use, and Political Participation'. *Communication Research* **38** (4): 451–470; Calenda, D., and A. Meijer. (2009). 'Young People, the Internet and Political Participation: Findings of a Web Survey in Italy, Spain and the Netherlands'. *Information, Communication & Society* **12** (6): 879–898.

52. Harlow, S. (2011). 'Social Media and Social Movements: Facebook and an Online Guatemalan Justice Movement that Moved Offline'. *New Media & Society* **14** (2): 225–243.

53. Norris (2004).

54. Cross, W., and L. Young. (2008). 'Factors Influencing the Decision of the Young Politically Engaged to Join a Political Party'. *Party Politics* **14** (3): 345–369. @ 346.

55. Farthing, R. (2010). 'The Politics of Youthful Antipolitics: Representing the "Issue" of Youth Participation in Politics'. *Journal of Youth Studies* **13** (2): 181–195.

56. Haste, H., and A. Hogan. (2006). 'Beyond Conventional Civic Participation, Beyond the Moral-Political Divide: Young People and Contemporary Debates about Citizenship'. *Journal of Moral Education* **35** (4): 473–493. @ 479.

57. O'Toole, T., M. *Lister*, D. Marsh, S. Jones, and A. McDonagh. (2003). 'Tuning Out or Left Out? Participation and Non-participation among Young People'. *Contemporary Politics* **9** (1): 45–61. @ 51.

58. Henn, M., and N. Foard. (2012). 'Young People, Political Participation and Trust in Britain'. *Parliamentary Affairs* **65** (1): 47–67. @ 49.

59. Skelton, T. (2010). 'Taking Young People as Political Actors Seriously: Opening the Borders of Political Geography'. *Area* **42** (2): 145–151. @ 147.

60. Flinders, M. (2015). 'The General Rejection? Political Disengagement, Disaffected Democrats and "Doing Politics" Differently'. *Parliamentary Affairs* **68** (suppl 1): 241–254.

61. Breindl, Y., and P. Francq. (2008). 'Can Web 2.0 Applications Save E-democracy? A Study of How New Internet Applications May Enhance Citizen Participation in the Political Process Online'. *International Journal of Electronic Democracy* **1** (1): 14–31.

62. Macintosh, A., E. Robson, E. Smith, and A. Whyte. (2003). 'Electronic Democracy and Young People'. *Social Science Computer Review* **21** (1):43–54.

63. Bennett, W. L (Ed). (2008). *Civic Life Online: Learning How Digital Media Can Engage Youth.* Cambridge, MA: MIT Press.

64. Loader, B. D., and D. Mercea. (2011). 'Networking Democracy?' *Information, Communication & Society* **14** (6): 757–769. @ 759.

65. Marichal, J. (2016). *Facebook Democracy: The Architecture of Disclosure and the Threat to Public Life.* London: Routledge.

66. Kim, J-Y. (2006). 'The Impact of Internet Use Patterns on Political Engagement: A Focus on Online Deliberation and Virtual Social Capital'. *Information Polity* **11** (1): 35–49. @ 47–48.

67. Fell, D., and Y.-W. Peng. (2016). 'The Electoral Fortunes of Taiwan's Green Party'. *Japanese Journal of Political Science* **17** (1): 63–83. @ especially 65–66.

68. Hayduk, R. (2012). 'Global Justice and OWS: Movement Connections'. *Socialism and Democracy* **26** (2): 43–50; Heynen, N. (2010). 'Cooking Up Non-violent Civil-Disobedient Direct Action for the Hungry: "Food Not Bombs" and the Resurgence of Radical Democracy in the US'. *Urban Studies* **47** (6): 1225–1240.

69. Sotirakopoulos, N., and G. Sotiropoulos. (2013). ' "Direct Democracy Now!": The Greek Indignados and the Present Cycle of Struggles'. *Current Sociology* **61** (4):

443–456; Juris, J. S., and G. H. Pleyers. (2009). 'Alter-Activism: Emerging Cultures of Participation among Young Global Justice Activists'. *Journal of Youth Studies* **12** (1): 57–75.

70. Servaes, J., and R Hoyng (2015). 'The Tools of Social Change: A Critique of Techno-centric Development and Activism'. *New Media & Society* online first. @ 5.

71. Thornberg, R., and H. Elvstrand. (2012). 'Children's Experiences of Democracy, Participation, and Trust in School'. *International Journal of Education Research* **53**: 44–54. @ 46.

72. Nam, C. (2012). 'Implications of Community Activism among Urban Minority Young People for Education for Engaged and Critical Citizenship'. *International Journal of Progressive Education* **8** (3): 62–76. @ 65.

73. Mitchell, K. (2007). 'Geographies of Identity: The Intimate Cosmopolitan'. *Progress in Human Geography* **31** (5): 706–720. @ 714.

74. Woodhouse, K. M. (2009). 'The Politics of Ecology: Environmentalism and Liberalism in the 1960s'. *Journal for the Study of Radicalism* **2** (2): 53–84.

75. Rosanvallon, P. (2008). *Counter-Democracy: Politics in an Age of Distrust.* Cambridge: Cambridge University Press.

76. Hytten, K. (2009). 'Deweyan Democracy in a Globalized World'. *Educational Theory* **59** (4): 395–408. @ 397.

77. Dewey, J. (1937). 'The Challenge of Democracy to Education'. In *John Dewey: The Later Works, 1925–1953* volume 11, edited by J. A. Boydston. Carbondale: Southern Illinois University Press. @ 182.

78. Minteer, B. A. (2005). 'Environmental Philosophy and the Public Interest: A Pragmatic Reconciliation'. *Environmental Values* **14** (1): 37–60. @ 47–48.

79. Ibid. @ 2.

80. Merkel, W. (2014). 'Is There a Crisis of Democracy?' *Democratic Theory* **1** (2): 11–25; Merkel, W., and J.-P. Gagnon. (2016). 'Democracies and Their Crises Reconsidered'. *Democratic Theory* **3** (1): 91–109.

81. Rosanvallon, P., and J.-P. Gagnon. 2014. 'Certain Turns of Modernity in Democratic Theory'. In J.-P. Gagnon, *Democratic Theorists in Conversation: Turns in Contemporary Thought.* London: Palgrave Macmillan. pp. 117–130. @ 128–130.

82. Hilbert, M. (2009). 'The Maturing Concept of E-Democracy: From E-voting and Online Consultations to Democratic Value out of Jumbled Online Chatter'. *Journal of Information Technology & Politics* **6** (2): 87–110.

83. Johnson, C., and B. Marshall. (2004). *'Political Engagement among Young People: An Update'.* Research Paper Prepared by the Electoral Commission. Available online: http://www.electoralcommission.org.uk/__data/assets/electoral_commission_pdf_file/0016/16135/Politicalengagementamongyoungpeople_14096-10669__E__N__S__W__.pdf. @ 8.

84. Hill, L., and S. Rutledge-Prior. (2016). 'Young People and Intentional Informal Voting in Australia'. *Australian Journal of Political Science* **51** (3): 400–417.

85. The literature on the dangers of not voting is compelling as, in both plurality and proportional electoral systems, less votes cast tends to accentuate the power of special interests of those who are politically active and who vote often. For more, see: Brennan, J. (2011). *The Ethics of Voting.* Princeton: Princeton University Press.

@ 1–7; Hamilton, L. H. (2016). *Congress, Presidents, and American Politics: Fifty Years of Writings and Reflections.* Bloomington: Indiana University Press. @ 284–286; McElwee, S. (2015). 'Why Voting Matters: Large Disparities in Turnout Benefit the Donor Class'. *Demos.* Available online: http://www.demos.org/publication/why-voting-matters-large-disparities-turnout-benefit-donor-class.

86. Wingenbach, E. (2011). *Institutionalizing Agonistic Democracy: Post-Foundationalism and Political Liberalism.* Farnham: Ashgate. @ xi; Schlosberg, D. (2006). 'The Pluralist Imagination'. In Dryzek, J. S., B. Honig, and A. Phillips (Eds). *The Oxford Handbook of Political Theory.* Oxford: Oxford University Press. pp. 142–162. @ 150.

Chapter Three

Civics and Citizenship Education

Defender or Divider of Democracy?

Catherine Hartung

The presence and enactment of citizenship permeates school life in all kinds of intended and unintended ways. Indeed, the shaping of citizens has been a fundamental purpose of education since at least the modern school system emerged in the nineteenth century.[1] Since then, citizenship education has expanded considerably, and so too young people's political engagement. While there are examples of citizenship education making a difference, the schools and organisations that produce and implement curricula and programmes can also create inadvertent barriers to participation for many young people. In the following chapter I explore popular understandings of citizenship education within schools and other institutions, highlighting the strengths and limitations of these programmes and initiatives, as well as suggesting possible ways forward in the pursuit of increased political engagement.

As demand for a more active citizenry has increased, debates regarding citizenship education have intensified among researchers, educators and policymakers. This has resulted in a proliferation of educational strategies and interventions to foster young people's active citizenship through state education policy, reports and national curricula, much of which focuses on young people developing skills, knowledge and values (e.g. flexibility, empathy, responsibility, interculturality, reflexivity, entrepreneurialism, resourcefulness) that are seen to allow young people to engage democratically in society. Approaches to citizenship in schools can take both formal and informal forms. Formal civics learning occurs through subjects (e.g. 'Civics and Citizenship' and 'Citizenship Studies'), whereas informal learning occurs through instrumental and expressive activities (e.g. student elections and representative committees).[2] These informal activities are considered by many to be 'among the best predictors of adult political engagement' compared with general social activities and sports.[3]

More so than any other educational priority, citizenship education asks young people to reflect on, and change, their cultural, political and social identities in accordance with particular democratic ideals. Underpinning such explanations are particular notions of rights and responsibilities, as well as notions of youth empowerment and voice. Such an offering challenges a deficit model of young people, a model that has received substantial criticism in the last forty years for excluding and dismissing young people's political agency because it presumes young people are too immature, incompetent, vulnerable or disobedient.

Kylie Smith, a child and youth researcher at the University of Melbourne, argues that citizenship education provides young people with an opportunity to learn about what it means to live in a democracy, including access to language and strategies to support engagement and experimentation.[4] Smith also believes that citizenship education enables educators, parents and governments to better understand 'the complexity and shifting nature of childhood and citizenship'.[5]

Given the growing interest in citizenship education in the twenty-first century, it may seem surprising that there is substantial disagreement regarding what works and how a young person's citizenship can or should be measured.[6] Typically, what tends to occur is a top-down approach to curriculum development and measurement, whereby panels of senior educators, experts and parliamentary committees determine the extent to which young people are engaging and will engage in the future as active citizens. For example, the International Association for the Evaluation of Educational Achievement (IEA) and Civic Education Study (CIVED) found that the culture of the school is a key indicator of whether or not a young person will be politically engaged.[7] Active participation at school was also seen as a common predictor of later civic engagement according to findings from the International Civic and Citizenship Education Study (ICCS) of secondary school students across thirty-eight countries.[8]

These evaluations of citizenship education can be useful in showing the prevalence of particular kinds of citizenship among young people. However, they can also inadvertently undermine young people's perspectives and forms of participation that do not fit neatly into institutionally driven notions of citizenship. In other words, evaluations can fail to recognise that young people are citizens who are 'already active—just in ways not always understood'.[9] Further, the evaluations fail to recognise context and the subtle processes of exclusion that occur within schools that privilege some students and forms of citizenship over others. Consequently, in this chapter I will begin by exploring what I mean by citizenship followed by an analysis of the strengths and limitations of popular approaches to citizenship education, before ending with some possible future directions.

YOUNG PEOPLE AS THE HEART OF DEMOCRACY?
CONTEXTUALISING CITIZENSHIP EDUCATION

It has long been argued that education is at the core of a successful democracy. As the Thirty-Second President of the United States, Franklin D. Roosevelt, once declared, 'Democracy cannot succeed unless those who express their choice are prepared to choose wisely. The real safeguard of democracy, therefore, is education'.[10] Unsurprisingly, the primary subjects of such democratic learning are young people, whose citizenship education is often declared 'the key to true democracy, a way to transform unjust decision-making structures so that every child's voice can be heard and their wishes acted upon'.[11] Such a view is premised on the assumption that a well-functioning representative democracy depends on citizens who are both informed of and active in the mechanisms of representative democracy. For both political scientists and civic educators, there is a commonly held conviction that if young people are taught the basic tenets of citizenship, democracy and the political institutions that govern them, they will not only be more politically savvy but will realise that it is in their best interest to actively participate in politics. After all, civics is about enabling youth to meaningfully participate in public life. This is because, conventionally defined, citizenship education has been geared towards helping young people to obtain knowledge about the political system and the attributes of good citizenship.[12] This is in large part why politicians and policymakers speak at length about the need to revitalise civics in school curricula. The two—inadequate citizenship education and youth ambivalence towards democracy—are seen as related.

At the heart of any interpretation of democracy are particular understandings of citizenship and the rights and duties of both young people and adults as citizens. Common conceptions of democracy in Anglo-American democracies are predicated on a principle of equality, whereby all citizens are not only subject and entitled to the same laws and opportunities but also have a right to a sense of belonging to society. Consequently, in order to understand how young people belong and contribute to democratic institutions it is valuable to understand the broader changes that have occurred in ideas of citizenship.[13]

Suggesting the opposite of passivity and indifference, 'active citizenship' is a highly appealing notion in many Western countries—especially the United States, the United Kingdom and Australia—where there are increasing concerns regarding voter apathy and welfare dependency.[14] The appeal of young people's citizenship, evident in the significant body of research on the topic, is that it provides practitioners and advocates with greater legitimacy by linking participatory practices with wider structures, spaces and objectives.[15] Although theoretically these structures, spaces and objectives can be social, political, cultural or economic, it is the political, or more specifically the democratic, that tend to receive the most attention.

Democratic understandings of citizenship consider it a useful way for marginalised groups to widen traditionally exclusive political spaces. Evelina Dagnino,[16] a Professor in Political Science at the University of Campinas, argues the notion of citizenship has become a 'crucial weapon' in combating exclusion and inequality, and also capable of 'widening of dominant conceptions of politics itself'. This weapon has the potential to challenge views of young people as helpless and incapable of making decisions regarding their own lives. Where once young people were excluded from governmental decisions, speaking about young people as citizens can, for example, create greater governmental accountability, encouraging decisions to be made with young people, rather than simply for them. Furthermore, it can create the basis for more inclusive practices that not only strengthen rights-based agendas but extend upon them.

In many ways the language of citizenship can help to move beyond tokenistic participatory processes with young people, whereby simply 'listening' to them is no longer seen as enough in implementing their citizenship rights. This means moving beyond 'giving children a say' and recognising different forms of young people's everyday participation and lived active citizenship.

The notion of young people's citizenship is often taken for granted and can be difficult to question; those who do can look heartless or morally bankrupt. As Invernizzi and Milne ask, '[H]ow far is the idea of children's citizenship becoming an essentially emotional issue which one scarcely dares to criticise'?[17] Drawing on this notion of young people's citizenship potentially allows for a redefinition of their participation that acknowledges the influence of context and larger-scale relations of power on practice. However, this is not always the case. And while the positive outcomes of framing young people's engagement through citizenship should not be underestimated, it is important to consider some of the potential limitations and contradictions. This is partly because young people's citizenship is a highly nebulous concept and encompasses an array of interrelated dimensions, from the political, moral, social and economic, to the environmental, critical, emotional and spiritual.

The meaning of the term 'citizenship' is context-dependent with the potential to be co-opted by a variety of different interest groups to serve competing needs. When young people are given the label 'citizens', their identities and behaviours become aligned with particular interest groups (whether it be those of the state, the school, the United Nations, NGOs or the academy). Where one group might be concerned with liberating young people from their present structural constraints, another might be more concerned with how young people may support, enhance or reproduce institutionally favourable practices and systems. This allows citizenship to operate as a 'social dividing line', between the 'active' and the 'inactive', the 'powerful' and the 'powerless', and adults and young people.[18]

Most would agree inclusion is a primary purpose of education, encompassing economic, political, cultural and personal aspects of belonging.[19] Yet, young people remain precariously placed in the democratic process with unequal access to citizenship's material and symbolic resources such as voting rights. Indeed, full citizenship is always somewhat of an impending proposition.[20] However, there is also an increasing demand to educate young people so that they can solve problems. For example, Walter Parker and colleagues[21] surveyed a multinational panel of 182 scholars, practitioners and policymakers from the fields of science and technology, health and education, politics and government, business, industry and the arts across United Kingdom, Europe, North America and Asia.[22] The survey, which aimed to inform and reshape school curriculum for the needs of the new millennium, found that the major perceived educational need was for 'multidimensional citizens' who were formed through a 'multinational, deliberation-based school curriculum focused on complex worldwide ethical problems'.[23] From this perspective, citizenship education has taken on a profound new meaning, simultaneously challenging an apparent civic deficit among young people while also positioning them as the solution to a host of societal ills, from graffiti at the local playground to climate change.

Citizenship education fundamentally intersects with what kind of future we wish to create or at least are willing to endure. Ennew argues that to deem a young person responsible for changing the structures within which their marginalisation is written 'reproduces the same inequalities in political and economic structures, while reinforcing the economic structures that produce and maintain inequalities'.[24] This can reinforce young people's sense of 'powerlessness' because the methods used in constituting the active citizen link an individual to their subjugation, and activism to discipline.[25] Further, the notion of citizenship can be used to privilege formal forms of political participation over informal or less formal practices.

Recognising that citizenship education can reinforce rather than overcome political exclusion does not mean that I should abandon the notion of citizenship altogether. However, it does suggest that I should avoid taking its influence at face value. I need to recognise its potential contradictions and complexities so that I can avoid excluding certain young people while privileging others. Questions remain regarding the construction of young people as both 'the problem to be solved' and 'the solution to the problem' as the juxtaposition of both perspectives creates a paradox. For how can young people make a problem for democratic citizenship but also simultaneously solve that problem? The paradox suggests that the reality of young people's political participation is more nuanced and complex, than what is described by the statements that they are democracy's 'problem-makers' and 'problem-solvers'.

CITIZENSHIP EDUCATION IN SCHOOLS:
INCLUSIONS AND EXCLUSIONS IN NEW TIMES

Citizenship is as much about who belongs as it is about who does not belong;[26] it is a site occupied by both 'entitled insiders and de-privileged outsiders'.[27] This is because state borders are always founded on the presumption of 'the other', against which a nation defines itself.[28] This inclusionary—exclusionary binary is reflected in current approaches to citizenship education, which has been 'rediscovered' as a major focus of policy and curriculum in Western democracies like the United Kingdom, the United States and Australia.

In the United Kingdom, young people have been the focus of a range of educational interventions in the past two decades based on a concern that schools are failing to politically engage young people. This was highlighted in the 1998 Crick Report that provided the impetus for a range of more recent interventions aimed at improving democratic behaviour among students. Yet there has been concern that the appealing rhetoric of citizenship education is far from the reality of schools. In a study of students and teachers from four English schools, two primary and two secondary, it was found that while citizenship was an increasingly explicit component of school syllabi, its interpretation was limited to young people's learning outcomes and was rarely used to support young people's participation in everyday school processes beyond the tokenistic. Specifically, the study found that the participation was tokenistic because while children were 'given a voice' they had very little control over the subject or style of communication and little chance to develop an opinion. Further, it was curriculum *products* that were emphasised, as opposed to the school *processes* that had a far greater influence in terms of facilitating participation.[29]

These findings are echoed in a number of studies that have questioned the effectiveness of school councils in the United Kingdom.[30] Veitch[31] argues that the dominant citizenship framework used within schools results in student participation being defined very broadly as 'taking part', which enables the legitimation of school councils as effective regardless of the significance or scale of their outcomes. However, when participation is defined in terms of its capacity for making the radical and transformative possible, school councils are viewed as tokenistic.

Addressing criticisms of tokenism, the United Kingdom's Department for Education decided to retain citizenship education as part of the National Curriculum, with a stronger focus on the promotion of links between the school and community to foster active citizenship. This is based on the belief that teaching and learning should recognise the diverse ways that citizens can contribute to the community, including volunteering.[32] Further, Osler and Starkley argue that contemporary citizenship education in the United Kingdom is a site for the promotion of diversity and social cohesion, as well as a site for debating issues of social upheaval, inclusion and equity.[33] They state 'the need for education designed to challenge inequality and injustice has been strengthened since 11 September 2001 because of a growing perception of links between poverty, injustice and inequality in the world and terrorist movements'.[34] However, the idea that young people should provide feedback to improve the school and wider community has also been critiqued due to its alignment with New Labour's neoliberal notion of active citizenship, whereby responsibility for challenging inequality shifts from the state to the individual.[35]

The recent revival of citizenship education in Australia reflects similar values and concerns to that of the United Kingdom. During the 1990s, due to concern regarding low levels of perceived political literacy and efficacy, the conservative government at the time introduced 'Discovering Democracy' (1997), a funding initiative to aid the development of curriculum resources and professional development for teachers regarding civics and citizenship. According to the Ministerial Statement, Discovering Democracy was not only concerned with developing young people's citizenship knowledge but their 'active citizenship', which, as with the U.K. policy, emphasised participation through volunteering and community service as well as learning to speak before bodies including school councils.[36] This led to many schools providing a range of activities for students, including student councils, school rallies and fundraising events for charity.

Terminated in 2004, Discovering Democracy is still considered the most significant initiative of its kind in Australia,[37] yet evaluations of its impact are at best mixed. Erebus Consulting found the initiative had an impact on teaching and learning, although only one-third of schools had developed participatory activities as part of the curriculum and this was put forward as an area for improvement.[38] The CIVED evaluation, conducted around the same time, compared Australia with schools around the world and found that young people's civic knowledge and confidence to participate at school met the global average, but that their attitude towards future participation in politics was far less positive. In a more critical take, Arvanitakis and Marren point to the results from the 2004 national testing of students that saw 92 per cent of Year Six students and 60 per cent of Year Ten students failing to meet minimum proficiency in civics and citizenship.[39] Arvanitakis and Marren argue these results demonstrate 'a key policy failure and misdirection of funds on the part of the Howard government in their attempts to revitalise civics education'.[40] These findings further prompted the move to a more participatory approach to citizenship education that has come to dominate much of the literature.[41]

Similarly, in her 2001 ethnographic study of a student engagement programme in an American high school in Berkeley, California, Silva highlights
the intersecting roles of race, ethnicity and class in shaping who was included
and who was excluded in a seemingly democratic process. Silva notes that
students are often aware of their own position within an invisible hierarchy,
quoting one Black student:

> We got squeaky wheels and flat tires . . . Some smooth white walls rollin' their
> way right to college, gettin' oil all the way. And then the rest of us . . . flat tires!
> Bumpin' on down the road, making all sorts of crude noises. Probably fall off
> real soon anyway. Ain't worth the grease.[42]

This quote highlights how 'having a voice' can mean very different things
depending upon a student's social and cultural background and their sense of
belonging. The closer a young person's connection to the pre-existing agenda
of the school, the more likely it was that the 'squeaky wheels' (predominantly
White females who were already high-achievers and confident verbal com-
municators involved in school activities) would come to dominate the group's
activities. For these students, it made sense to voice their opinions within the
school's terms. As Silva argues, 'they had experienced success through coop-
eration with the school's rules and policies, it seemed appropriate to them for
the group to behave in a similar, more conformist manner'.[43]

For other students, however, including those that associated themselves as
'flat tires' and 'students of color from neighboring, poorer communities, and
those with the lowest levels of achievement', conforming to more formal and
school-determined processes was problematic. For these students, having a
voice was understood very differently, 'incited by their desire to disturb the
traditional decision-making and reform process of the school, not to be a part
of it'. One Black student who decided to pull out of the group explained: 'I
just have my own priorities right now. They [student outreach] have some
good ideas, but I'm not so much about empowering the school. I'm more
about empowering myself and my people'.[44]

Arguably, this issue of exclusion in citizenship education is not unique to
Silva's case study. Indeed, this story is reflective of many schools and educational systems across the globe that fail to recognise the Eurocentricity and
colonial logics that underpin understandings of national and global citizenship.[45] For Olson, such an approach to citizenship education involves a 'fixed
set of nationally encompassing moral skills and values' that form a 'resi-
denced democracy', rendering alternative forms of citizenship incompatible,
unrecognisable or 'not-yets'.[46] In this way, citizenship education is narrowly
focused on teaching young people skills and knowledge related to citizenship
as an apprenticeship in particular conceptions of democracy, disregarding the

ways in which young people in different cultural contexts actively participate politically in their everyday lives.[47]

Underpinning this approach to citizenship education is an image of what a responsible young citizen *should* look like, and by implication, what they *don't* look like. Schools, as governing institutions, contain their own norms and rules about how young people should act that can privilege those young people whose behaviour and academic performance meets expectations while overlooking those 'voices from the margins'[48] that fail to comply; 'those that seem incomprehensible, recalcitrant or even obnoxious'.[49] It is no accident that student representative committees tend to be made up of the 'best and brightest'; those 'good' students whose exceptional academic performance, social popularity, 'will to participate' and/or cultural capital make them appealing to leadership positions yet far from representative of the 'cacophony of competing voices'[50] in a diverse student population. Further, as Bragg points out, it is understandable that many young people choose not to participate in this work in schools, indeed some 'might feel that school has not given them anything, just as learning and employability are social not just individual issues'.[51]

Yet such a critique of young people's participation in democratic processes within the school is not new. For example, feminist writers questioned the hidden agenda behind educational uses of student voice and participation more than two decades ago.[52] These criticisms were echoed and extended in the late 1990s and early 2000s. For example, Fielding's review of student participatory initiatives in U.K. schools in the 1990s asked if the emergence was 'genuinely new, exciting and emancipatory' or in fact further entrenching existing assumptions that use young people's participation 'as an additional mechanism of control'.[53] Yet, such concerns often go unnoticed as the field of citizenship education grows to include a number of new stakeholders outside the field of education.

CITIZENSHIP EDUCATION BEYOND THE SCHOOL: THE NEW GLOBAL AUTHORITIES

Schools are not the only institutions with an investment in citizenship education and the production of young people as responsible democratic citizens. An increasing number of non-government and transnational organisations are not only taking an interest in citizenship education but are emerging as key 'global authorities' on the subject. These organisations are part of a wider institutional network that is moving beyond local and national borders in the protection, education and governance of young people.

The United Nations, in particular, has emerged as a global authority in relation to young people's citizenship education, especially through the work of the United Nations Children's Fund (UNICEF) and United Nations Educational, Scientific and Cultural Organisation (UNESCO). UNICEF was originally set up to provide services and supplies to war-affected children; however, towards the end of the twentieth century this slowly shifted to a view of the young person as an active citizen, solidified with the almost universal ratification of the United Nations Convention on the Rights of the Child (UNCRC) in 1989. The UNCRC emphasises young people's political freedoms and right to participate in decision-making alongside their rights to protection and provision of basic services. It recognises young people's active membership within the family, communities and wider society and their right to:

- 'express their views on all matters affecting them and for their views to be taken seriously' (Article 12);
- 'freedom of expression, including freedom to seek, receive, and impart information and ideas of all kinds through any media they choose' (Article 13); and
- 'education that promotes children's emotional, intellectual, and physical development; that fosters awareness and understanding of parents' roles and of the importance of cultural identity, language, and values; and that prepares children for a responsible life in society' (Article 29).

The adoption of the UNCRC by UNICEF represented a fundamental shift from a focus on welfare to a rights discourse that provided a powerful framework in which to view children and young people internationally, stripping away the limited and less persuasive welfare discourse that had previously dominated. This also led to the development of children's rights research and education centres and networks, with the wide dissemination of various publications such as UNICEF's Innocenti Research Centre and State of the World's Children (SOWC) Reports that present national statistics on children's wellbeing and rights. UNICEF have also developed a variety of teaching materials and programmes relevant to citizenship educators available through their TeachUNICEF website,[54] which states that 'through a focus on global citizenship and child rights, TeachUNICEF engages students in an exploration of humanitarian issues and inspires them to take action to improve their world'. Similarly, UNESCO provides a multitude of education resources focused on citizenship and global citizenship in particular. Indeed, it is rare to find a document on global citizenship education that does not make reference to their work.

Alongside, and often in collaboration with, UNICEF and UNESCO are numerous NGOs with an increasing investment in young people's education and citizenship (e.g. Save the Children, Plan International, ChildFund, Bernard van Leer Foundation, World Vision, Amnesty International, Peace Child International, Childwatch International and Eurochild). Most of these organisations originated in Europe and the United Kingdom in the early to mid-twentieth century, though it was not until the 1980s that the impact of NGOs really began to accelerate on an international level. This reflects the wider 'associational revolution' witnessed in international development during the 1980s.[55] As Cornwall describes, 'a consensus emerged that smaller-scale organisations with relative autonomy from the state were better placed to operationalize what came to be known as "people's participation"'.[56] Similarly, Henkel and Stirrate argue that the rise of the NGO reflects a 'distrust of the state' that positions NGOs as 'somehow more "efficient" than state bodies'.[57] This emphasis on efficiency is evident, for example, in Save the Children's 2010–2015 global strategy that aims to 'dramatically increase the scope and scale' of their education programmes in 120 countries by merging this with their health and protection programmes into one management structure; a change which was seen to enable Save the Children to be 'even more efficient and accountable to children'.[58]

The rise of NGOs, coupled with the work of the United Nations, has had significant effects on citizenship education and young people who have consequently become the *object* of the 'development mainstream'.[59] The UNCRC in particular has cemented the discursive reference point for these NGOs, although many were at the forefront of producing and disseminating knowledge about children and young people's rights and citizenship well before the construction and ratification of the UNCRC.[60] This growing interconnectedness has enabled these NGOs to become global authorities on what it means to be a young citizen and how to educate for citizenship. However, the involvement of NGOs in the production of knowledge about young people is complex and limited. For example, given the geographical location of many of these NGOs, the knowledge produced and disseminated privileges western modes of citizenship that potentially exclude other modes of citizenship in the Global South. Further, given that NGOs are increasingly reliant on the private sector, the state, the United Nations and the academy to stay globally influential and financially viable, it is inevitable that their objectives will be compromised or at least shaped by their supporters' competing agendas.

Nonetheless, networks of NGOs and UN agencies have increasingly endowed themselves with the means for not only advocating, protecting and providing for young people, but with the task of educating, monitoring and assessing. This can be seen in the increasing number of international agreements, laws and regulations, as well as research publications, initiatives and campaigns that establish rules pertaining to the ways in which young people are educated and governed as citizens.

A major effect of increasingly influential networks of NGOs and UN agencies is that citizenship education is becoming organised and managed according to institutionally-preferred outcomes, monitored and measured through legislation, reports and publications by a range of global stakeholders. Since the 1990s, notions of measurement, efficiency, accountability, outcomes and evaluation have become central to welfare services.[61] In turn, such terms have received increasing interest from NGOs and the United Nations, influencing the kind of knowledge they produce and disseminate. Through its association with these supporters, citizenship education is increasingly defined as something to be monitored and regulated in accordance with a range of institutional agendas. This in turn creates pressure to produce and disseminate knowledge shorn of nuance, complexity, the unexpected and the frustrating. In particular, managerially-driven practices can downplay or even exclude the role of emotions in participatory relationships. Indeed, the emotional might even be viewed as weak or problematic in organisations that prioritise what is measurable and manageable.[62]

Consequently, the pressure to produce rapid and measurable outcomes may both dehumanise and de-contextualise young people's citizenship and education. Not only is this knowledge de-contextualised, but for the purposes of dissemination, it is re-contextualised in new institutionally-preferred spaces. While these more immediate, accessible or tangible versions of citizenship may be productive and useful for young people, taking the time with the ambiguous, the affective, the unexpected or the inconsistent in young people's citizenship can offer possibilities for expanding beyond these limitations. Seeking and understanding young people's everyday experiences of citizenship is an important and necessary step. In the final section of this chapter, I consider alternative conceptualisations of citizenship education and how a closer understanding of young people's views and practices might allow for a more inclusive approach to citizenship education.

BEYOND EDUCATION FOR SOCIALISATION: YOUNG PEOPLE'S CITIZENSHIP AS PRACTICE

The above examples of citizenship education in and outside of schools reflect what Lawy describes as citizenship-as-achievement that focuses on improving the socialisation of young people for the benefit of society through effective schooling.[63] The problem with a focus on citizenship-as-achievement is that it inadvertently shifts responsibility from systems onto young people who are given responsibility for solving the world's problems. This focus works to constitute young people in accordance with their institutional value. There is an assumption that the world in which young people want to live and work will accord with an economic growth-oriented world and that the purpose of education is simply to shape a young person's behaviour in accordance with this worldview. This individualises the problem of young people's citizenship as well as citizenship in general, whereby there is also an assumption that good citizenship is a natural effect of a young person developing the correct skills, knowledge and dispositions.[64] This prevents or ignores different understandings of education and young people who may not be able, or desire, to fit into this image of citizen.

An uncritical focus on the individual responsibilities of young citizens also has the potential to *depoliticise* citizenship education and vice versa. This means that current policy and public debates that claim a lack of civic engagement among young people lead to claims for the need to increase participation in specific democratic institutions, and in turn a particular form of citizenship education is privileged. This simultaneously positions education as the solution to a civic deficit as well as affirming the assumption that education is capable of solving social and political problems.[65] Without critically engaging with the taken-for-grantedness of citizenship and citizenship education, we run the risk of reproducing rather than overcoming social and political inequality and disengagement.

Lawy proposes a role for education beyond this socialising function towards the notion of 'citizenship-as-practice'.[66] Citizenship-as-practice is oriented in the present rather than the future and based on the premise that young people's citizenship is 'shaped through their daily experiences within particular social, economic, institutional, political and historical contexts'.[67] From this perspective, a young person's civic identity is not essentialised or predetermined but 'mutable and constructed within different and varied social practices and contexts' with an 'action orientation that is located in the here-and-now where democratic and non-democratic practices are performed'.[68] This recognises that any citizen, regardless of age, is always in a process of becoming a citizen, and in doing so shifts the focus of citizenship education from outcomes and achievements and being a good citizen to a focus on 'action and interaction'.[69] This fits within what Isin describes as acts of citizenship which recognise forms of citizenship that are not tied to the institutional but collective and individual actions.[70] When merged with adjectives such as 'intimate', 'multicultural', 'sexual', 'ecological', 'transgendered' and 'consumer', new potential identities are formed that allow for 'new subjects, sites and scales of claim making'.

So what are some examples of young people's collective and individual actions as citizens that are not but could be incorporated into educational contexts? There is a body of literature that seeks to inform and improve citizenship education by drawing on interviews and focus groups with young people. However, much of this work presupposes particular kinds of appropriate citizenship and seeks to fit young people's views within these predetermined categories.[71] In recent years there has been a move to a more open-ended consideration of young people's articulation of citizenship and what it means to be a 'good citizen'.[72]

One notable exception is a U.K. longitudinal study by Lister and colleagues who identified five overlapping discourses regarding the 'good citizen' from their interviews with young people. The most common response related to 'universal status', followed by respectable economic independence, constructive social participation, social-contractual and right to a voice. Interestingly, formal forms of volunteering in the community, a cornerstone of traditional citizenship education, was one of the least mentioned activities (less than 10 per cent) of a good citizen. Instead, two-thirds of the young people interviewed emphasised a more general and informal keeping an eye out for others, 'a considerate and caring attitude towards others and a constructive approach towards and active participation in the community'.[73] As one young interviewee stated:

> I wouldn't call a good citizen like the kind who goes out to do charity and trying to raise money. That's not my version of a good citizen. Mine's like they'll help you out. They'll lend you something if you need it, and that's the way I see a good citizen . . . It's like your neighbours.

Listening to young people's perspectives on citizenship, especially those whose perspectives are often missing from the debate, challenges assumptions about what young people are invested in and offers a 're-imagining of the boundaries of the subject'.[74] Too often young people are only heard in predetermined or accepted roles like redesigning skate parks and school murals, that is, spaces where young people's voices are not complicated by their relationship to 'others'.[75] It is important to recognise that formal education is only one source of learning for young people and its position may become increasingly marginal, reduced to a instrumental credentialing apparatus for getting into university and employment.[76]

In Bessant, Farthing and Watts' study of young people, democratic deficit and political renewal in the EU, they describe how young people have 'established new approaches to using digital networks involving the re-imagining of politics and constituting new political imaginaries and new kinds of political action oriented to new forms of free non-hierarchical interaction'.[77] This politics is highly interactive, peer-based and not always concerned with hierarchies and authority, blends the cultural and expressive with the political and also involves a critique of the political consensus.

So what might a curriculum better informed by young people look like? Bessant, Farthing and Watts propose a 'co-design principle', a concept that can be traced back to the work of popular education philosopher John Dewey in the earlier part of the twentieth century.[78] While conscious not to become too prescriptive, they outline five protocols: recruiting participants, identifying and overcoming obstacles, the practice of enquiry and deliberation, clarity about the purpose, and obligations. They see this as a valuable project because it 'harvests and builds on knowledge and skills in ways that affirm the status of young people as moral and political agents'[79] while simultaneously informing policymakers about the political activities of young people that challenge the unsubstantiated and harmful stereotypes of young people as apolitical, narcissistic or disinterested in civics.

This radical vision sees education, not as a space of preparation, but a space where young people can as subjects 'bring their beginnings into the world'. This shifts the educational debate from a focus on how to produce democratic citizens to the multitude of ways young people, and individuals in general, can be subjects.[80]

This chapter has explored popular approaches to citizenship education as a way of overcoming a perceived civic deficit among young people. It has highlighted the dominant view within education circles that citizenship education is fundamentally about improving the socialisation of young people through better policy initiatives and curriculum. While there are clearly many benefits to this, the above analysis has highlighted significant limitations. There is an assumption that increasing civic engagement among young people is a matter of *more* or *better* citizenship education so that young people become good citizens as institutionally defined. This places the impetus on young people to strengthen democracy and solve a variety of societal problems while downplaying structural and systemic processes that can limit or open up possibilities.

Approaches to citizenship education that are heavily normalising have the potential to exclude those young people that do not fit the mould in accordance with the institution. Yet, the purpose of highlighting these limitations is not to suggest that the socialisation function of citizenship education is wrong or useless. Nor is it suggesting that I should add another subject to a congested curriculum. A curriculum that is responsive to the challenges faced by young people and society generally is not achieved by 'simply adding more dimensions to an already overloaded curriculum'.[81] Rather, the purpose is to help foster an openness to recognising alternatives.[82] In doing so I encourage a move beyond a focus on producing individuals that meet a particular criteria of a 'good citizen', stemming as it does from particular understandings of democracy as shown in the previous chapter, to recognise the variety of ways young people are already engaging in acts of citizenship. Such acts will be explored in the chapters to come.

NOTES

1. Friedrich, D. (2010). 'Historical consciousness as a pedagogical device in the production of the responsible citizen'. *Discourse: Studies in the Cultural Politics of Education* **31** (5): 649–663.

2. Print, M. (2009). 'Civic engagement and political education of young people'. *Minority Studies* **1** (3): 63–83.

3. Reichert, F. (2016). 'Learning for active citizenship: are Australian youths Discovering Democracy at school?' *Education, Citizenship and Social Justice*, **11** (2): 1–15. @ 3.

4. Smith, K. (2015). Childhood and youth citizenship. In J. Wyn and H. Cahill (Eds.) *Handbook of Children and Youth Studies.* Singapore: Springer Reference. 357–376. DOI 10.1007/978-981-4451-15-4_62

5. Ibid. @ 369.

6. See, for example, Ireland, E., D. Kerr, J. Lopes, J. Nelson, and E. Cleaver (2006). Active citizenship and young people: opportunities, experiences and challenges in and beyond school citizenship education longitudinal study: fourth annual report. National Foundation for Education Research, Report 732, Department of Education and Skills, London.

7. Torney-Purta, J., Lehmann, R., Oswald, H., et al. (2001). *Citizenship and Education in Twenty-Eight Countries: Civic Knowledge and Engagement at Age Fourteen.* Amsterdam: IEA.

8. Schultz, W., Ainley, J., Fraillon, J., et al. (2010). *ICCS 2009 International Report: Civic Knowledge, Attitudes, and Engagement among Lower-Secondary School Students in 38 Countries.* Amsterdam: IEA.

9. Arvanitakis, J. and Marren, S. (2009). *Putting the Politics Back into Politics: Young People and Democracy in Australia.* Discussion Paper, Sydney, The Whitlam Institute. @ 3.

10. Roosevelt, F. D. (1938). Message for American Education Week. September 27. Online by G. Peters and J. Woolley, *The American Presidency Project*. http://www.presidency.ucsb.edu/ws/?pid=15545

11. Gallagher, M. (2008). 'Foucault, power and participation'. *International Journal of Children's Rights* **16**: 395–406. @ 404.

12. Torney-Purta, J. (2004). 'Adolescents' political socialization in changing contexts: an international study in the spirit of Nevitt Sanford'. *Political Psychology* **25** (3): 465–478.

13. Cockburn, T. (2010). Children and deliberative democracy in England. In B. Percy-Smith and N. Thomas (Eds.), *A Handbook of Children and Young People's Participation: Perspectives from Theory and Practice.* New York: Routledge. 306–317.

14. See, for example, Cockburn, T. (2010). Children and deliberative democracy in England. In B. Percy-Smith and N. Thomas, *A Handbook of Children and Young People's Participation: Perspectives from Theory and Practice.* New York: Routledge. 306–317.

15. See, for example: Theis, J. (2010). Children as active citizens: an agenda for children's civil rights and civic participation. In B. Percy-Smith and N. Thomas (Eds.), *A Handbook of Children and Young People's Participation: Perspectives from Theory and Practice.* New York: Routledge. 343–355; Thomas, N. (2007). Towards a theory of children's participation. *International Journal of Children's Rights* 15: 199–218; Lister, R. (2006). *Investing in the citizen-workers of the future: Transformations in citizenship and the state under New Labour. The Welfare State Reader.* 455; Bessell, S. (2006). *Children, human rights and social policy: is citizenship the way forward? Crawford School of Economics and Government Seminar Series*, Australian National University, Canberra; Invernizzi, A. and B. Milne (2005). 'Children's citizenship: an emergent discourse on the rights of the child?' *Journal of Social Sciences* Special Issue no. 9; Wyness, M. (2001) 'Children, childhood and political participation: case studies of young people's councils'. *The International Journal of Children's Rights.* **9** (3): 193–212; Ennew, J. (2000). 'How can we define citizenship in childhood?' In R. Ranjani (Ed.), *The Political Participation of Children.* Harvard Center for Population and Development Studies.

16. Dagnino, E. (2005). ' "We all have rights, but . . ." Contesting concepts of citizenship'. In Brazil. In N. Kabeer (Ed.), *Inclusive Citizenship.* London: Zed Books. @ 150.

17. Invernizzi, A. and B. Milne (2005). 'Children's citizenship: an emergent discourse on the rights of the child?' *Journal of Social Sciences* Special Issue no. 9. @ 2.

18. de Winter, M. (1997). *Children as Fellow Citizens: Participation and Commitment.* Oxford and New York: Radcliffe Medical Press. @ 30.

19. Arnot, M. and Swartz, S. (2012). 'Youth citizenship and the politics of belonging: introducing contexts, voices, imaginaries'. *Comparative Education* **48** (1): 1–10.

20. Barnett, C., and Low, M. (2004). Introduction: Geography and Democracy. In C. Barnett and M. Low (Eds.), *Spaces of Democracy: Geographical Perspectives on Citizenship, Participation and Representation.* 1–22. London: Sage Publications.

21. Parker, W. C., A. Ninomiya and J. J. Cogan (2002). Educating 'world citizens': toward multinational curriculum development. In W. C. Parker (Ed.), *Education for Democracy: Contexts, Curricula, Assessments.* Greenwich, CT: Information Age Publishing. 151–184.

22. Specifically, the United Kingdom, the Netherlands, Hungary, Germany, Greece, Canada, the United States, Japan and Thailand.

23. Ibid. @ 162.

24. Ennew, J. (2000). How can we define citizenship in childhood? In R. Ranjani (Ed.), *The Political Participation of Children.* Harvard Center for Population and Development Studies. @ 5.

25. Brin Hyatt, S. (1997). Poverty in a 'post-welfare' landscape: tenant management policies, self-governance and the democratisation of knowledge in Great Britain. In C. Shore and S. Wright (Eds.), *The Anthropology of Policy: Critical Perspectives on Governance and Power.* 217–238. London: Routledge.

26. Shaheed, F. (2007). Citizenship and the nuanced belonging of women. In J. Bennet (Ed.), *Scratching the Surface: Democracy, Traditions, Gender.* 23–38. Lahore: Heinrich Boll Foundation.

27. Eckert, J. (2011). 'Introduction: subjects of citizenship'. *Citizenship Studies* **15** (3–4): 309–317. @ 311.

28. Spencer, P. and H. Wollman (2002). *Nationalism: A Critical Introduction*, Sage.

29. Wyse, D. (2001). 'Felt tip pens and school councils: children's participation rights in four English schools'. *Children & Society* **15** (4): 209–218.

30. For example, Veitch, H. (2009). 'Participation in practice: an evaluation of the primary school council as a participatory tool'. *Childhoods Today* **Special Issue** (June 21): 1–24.

31. Ibid.

32. Department for Education UK (2013). National curriculum in England: citizenship programmes of study for key stages 3 and 4. https://www.gov.uk/government/publications/national-curriculum-in-england-citizenship-programmes-of-study

33. Osler, A., and H. Starkey. (2006). 'Education for democratic citizenship: a review of research, policy and practice 1995–2005'. *Research Papers in Education* **21** (4): 433–466.

34. Ibid. @ 6.

35. Whitty, G., and Whisby, M. (2007). 'Whose voice? An exploration of the current interest in pupil involvement in school decision-making'. *International Studies in Sociology of Education* **17** (3): 303–319.

36. Kemp, D. (1997). *Discovering Democracy: Civics and Citizenship Education. A Ministerial Statement*. Canberra, ACT, Australia: Commonwealth of Australia.

37. Hughes, A. S, Print, M., and Sears, A., (2010). 'Curriculum capacity and citizenship education: a comparative analysis of four democracies'. *Compare* **40** (3): 293–309.

38. Erebus Consulting Partners, (2003). Evaluation of the Discovering Democracy Programme 2000–2003. A report to the Australian Government Department of Education, Science and Training. Canberra, ACT, Australia: DEST.

39. Arvanitakis, J. and Marren, S. (2009). *Putting the Politics Back into Politics: Young People and Democracy in Australia.* Discussion Paper, Sydney: The Whitlam Institute. @ 16.

40. Ibid.

41. See, for example, DeJaeghere, J. G., and Tudball, L. (2007). 'Looking back, looking forward: critical citizenship as a way ahead for civics and citizenship education in Australia'. *Citizenship Teaching and Learning* **3** (2): 40–57. Also Print, M. (2007). 'Citizenship education and youth participation in democracy'. *British Journal of Educational Studies* **55** (3): 325–345.

42. Silva, E. M., (2001). 'Squeaky wheels and flat tires: a case study of students as reform participants'. *Forum* **43** (2): 95–99. @ 95.

43. Ibid. @ 96.

44. Student cited, Ibid. @ 97.

45. See chapter 4 for a closer examination of global citizenship.

46. Olson, M. (2009). 'Democratic citizenship—A conditioned apprenticeship. A call for destabilisation of democracy in education'. *Journal of Social Science Education* **8** (4): 75–80. @ 77.

47. Blanchet-Cohen, N., and Torres, J. (2015). Enhancing citizen engagement at the municipal level: youth's perspectives. In J. Wyn and H. Cahill (Eds.) *Handbook of Children and Youth Studies.* 391–404. DOI 10.1007/978-981-4451-15-4_62

48. Wierenga, A. (2003). *Sharing a new story: young people in decision-making. Australian Youth Research Centre*, Working Paper 23. Melbourne: Foundation for Young Australians. @ 25.

49. Bragg, S. (2001). 'Taking a joke: learning from the voices we don't want to hear'. *Forum*, **43** (2): 70–73. @ 7.

50. Reay, D. (2006). '"I'm not seen as one of the clever children": consulting primary school pupils about the social conditions of learning'. *Educational Review* **58** (2): 171–181. @ 109.

51. Bragg, S. (2001). 'Taking a joke: learning from the voices we don't want to hear'. *Forum*, **43** (2): 70–73. @ 7.

52. See, for example: Ellsworth, E. (1989). 'Why doesn't this feel empowering? Working through the repressive myths of critical pedagogy'. *Harvard Educational Review* **59**: 297–324; Gore, J. M. (1991). 'On silent regulation: emancipatory action research in preservice teacher education'. *Curriculum Perspectives* **11** (4): 47–51; Orner, M. (1992). Interrupting the call for students' voice in liberatory education: a feminist poststructuralist perspective. In C. Luke and J. Gore (Eds.) *Feminisms and Critical Pedagogy*. 74–90. London: Routledge.

53. Fielding, M. (2001). 'Beyond the rhetoric of student voice: new departures or new constraints in the transformation of 21st century schooling?' *Forum* 43. @ 100.

54. TeachUNICEF (n.d.) TeachUNICEF website. teachunicef.org. Accessed online: 23 July 2016.

55. Salamon, L. (1993). *The Global Associational Revolution: The Rise of the Third Sector on the World Scene.* Baltimore: John Hopkins University. @ 1.

56. Cornwall, A. (2006). Historical perspectives on participation in development. *Commonwealth & Comparative Politics* **44** (1): 62–83. @ 74.

57. Henkel, H. and R. Stirrat (2001). Participation as spiritual duty: empowerment as secular subjection. In B. Cooke and U. Kothari, *Participation: The New Tyranny?* London, Zed Books. 168–184. @ 171.

58. Save the Children (2010) *Global Strategy 2010–2015*. Save the Children.

59. Cornwall, A. (2006). Historical perspectives on participation in development. *Commonwealth & Comparative Politics* **44** (1): 62–83. @ 75.

60. For example, some consider Save the Children's founder Eglantyne Jebb the first to recognise children's rights and her early work is cited in the 1959 Declaration. Although Key's book *The Century of the Child* also recognised that children 'have duties and rights that are just as firmly established as those of their parents'. Ref: Key, E, (1900). *The Century of the Child.* New York: Arno Press. @ 199.

61. Hoggett, P. (2000). Social policy and the emotions. In G. Lewis, S. Gewirtz and J. Clarke, *Rethinking Social Policy*. 141–153. London: Open University/Sage.

62. Pinkney, S. (2005). *Competing constructions of children's participation in social care: analysing text and talk. PhD thesis*. Milton Keynes: Open University.

63. Lawy, R. (2014). 'Education beyond socialisation: on becoming and being a citizen-subject in everyday life'. *Discourse: Studies in the Cultural Politics of Education* **35** (4): 599–610.

64. Biesta, G. and Lawy, R. (2006). 'From teaching citizenship to learning democracy: Overcoming individualism in research, policy and practice'. *Cambridge Journal of Education*, **36** (1): 63–79. doi:10.1080/03057640500490981

65. Nicoll, K, Fejes, A., Olson, M., Dahlstedt, M., and Biesta, G. (2013). 'Opening discourses of citizenship education: a theorization with Foucault'. *Journal of Education Policy*, DOI: 10.1080/02680939.2013.823519

66. Lawy, R. (2014). 'Education beyond socialisation: on becoming and being a citizen-subject in everyday life'. *Discourse: Studies in the Cultural Politics of Education* **35** (4): 599–610. @ 601.

67. Rubin, B. C. (2007). '"There's still not justice": Youth civic identity development amid distinct school community contexts'. *Teachers College Record*, 109: 449–481. @ 478.

68. Lawy, R. (2014). 'Education beyond socialisation: on becoming and being a citizen-subject in everyday life'. *Discourse: Studies in the Cultural Politics of Education* **35** (4): 599–610. @ 602.

69. Ibid. @ 603.

70. Isin, E. (2008). Theorizing acts of citizenship. In E. Isin and G. Nielsen (Eds.) *Acts of Citizenship.* 15–43. London, Palgrave Macmillan. @ 17.

71. Nicoll, K, Fejes, A., Olson, M., Dahlstedt, M., and Biesta, G. (2013). 'Opening discourses of citizenship education: a theorization with Foucault'. *Journal of Education Policy*, DOI: 10.1080/02680939.2013.823519

72. See, for example:Ekman, T. (2007). *Democratic Competence: Upper Secondary School as a School for Democracy.* Goteborg: Goteborg University Press; Niklasson, L. (2007). *The Citizen as a Pedagogical Project.* Stockholm, Stockholm University Press; Olson, M. (2012). 'What counts as young people's civic engagement in times of accountability? On the importance of maintaining openness about young people's civic engagement in education'. *Education & Democracy* **21** (1): 29–55; Farthing, R. (2010). 'The politics of youthful antipolitics: representing the "issue" of youth participation in politics'. *Journal of Youth Studies* **13** (2): 181–195; Dahlgren, P. (2013). *The Political Web.* London, Palgrave Macmillan.Bessant, J. (2014). 'A dangerous idea? Freedom, children and the capability approach to education'. *Critical Studies in Education*, 55, 138–153.

73. Lister, R., N. Smith, S. Middleton, and L. Cox. (2003). 'Young people talk about citizenship: empirical perspectives on theoretical and political debates'. *Citizenship Studies* **7** (2): 235–253. @ 244.

74. Ruddick, S. (2007). 'At the horizons of the subject: neo-liberalism, neo-conservatism and the rights of the child. Part one: from "knowing" fetus to "confused" child'. *Gender, Place & Culture* **14** (5): 513–527. @ 515.

75. Ibid.

76. Wyn, J. (2009). *Touching the Future: Building Skills for Life and Work. Australian Council for Educational Research.* Camberwell, Australia: Australian Council for Educational Research.

77. Bessant, J., Farthing, R., and Watts, R. (2015). 'Co-designing a civics curriculum: young people, democratic deficit and political renewal in the EU'. *Journal of Curriculum Studies* 1–19. DOI: 10.1080/00220272.2015.1018329. @ 7.

78. Ibid.

79. Ibid. @ 10.

80. Biesta, G. (2006). *Beyond Learning: Democratic Education for a Human Future.* London: *Paradigm.* 137–138. @ 137–138.

81. Wyn, J. (2009). *Touching the Future: Building Skills for Life and Work. Australian Council for Educational Research.* Camberwell, Australia: Australian Council for Educational Research. @ 35.

82. Nicoll, K, Fejes, A., Olson, M., Dahlstedt, M., and Biesta, G. (2013). 'Opening discourses of citizenship education: a theorization with Foucault'. *Journal of Education Policy*, DOI: 10.1080/02680939.2013.823519

Chapter Four

Different Ways, Different Domains

The Everyday Politics of Young People

Lesley J. Pruitt

Curriculum experts and policymakers have long been concerned with their perception of young people exhibiting a 'civic deficit' or as citizens-in-the-making.[1] Yet, and as the previous three chapters have shown, there is now a growing body of scholarship demonstrating that young people are not as disengaged and deficient as previous reports have suggested.[2] Rather, there is a need to explore both traditional and non-traditional modes of political engagement amongst young people. As twelve-year-old American activist Abby Goldberg puts it: 'I tell other kids to use being a kid to their advantage. I know a lot about social media, I have a lot of friends and I have time to get involved. Actually I think it is our job to tell the adults about problems in the world. Sometimes adults are too busy to see all the problems'. She makes some important points. After all, while youth are afforded little to no say in formal political processes, they are not politically apathetic as is typically suggested in the mainstream politics literature. Instead, young people are practicing politics and exploring everyday understandings of citizenship in their own communities and networks. In this way, rather than seeing youth as disengaged, recent scholarship to which this book aims to contribute demonstrates how youth might engage in an ongoing process of citizenship, as they practice and enact citizenship through their everyday lives, both formally and informally.

This chapter explores and assesses the semi-formal and informal ways youth are learning about and participating politically to enable us to better examine whether young people are actually disengaging from politics and democracy, or whether—as chapter two suggests—they are only disengaging from certain practices of politics and democracy. Drawing from scholarship that employs alternative approaches that go beyond traditional notions of what political participation is or should be when looking at notions of citizenship and democracy, this chapter thus explores non-electoral and non-traditional domains of society where young people interact politically.[3]

The remainder of this chapter is structured as follows: First, I make a case for young people as vital to democracy, both present and future. Next, I explore how states enact a 'politics of concern' around young people, democracy and citizenship, which problematises the impact of young people. Then I identify and critically analyse ways governments attempt to engage and direct young people in democratic practice, particularly through school-based citizenship education. From there, I consider what young people do care about and how they already participate, sometimes in new, 'everyday'[4] ways and situate this alongside school-based initiatives, semi-formal participation and governmental, formal initiatives for civic involvement, both 'real' and 'virtual'. Finally, I consider caveats and complications to the points made, taking into account the current neoliberal political environment in the advanced democracies discussed before concluding with a reiteration of main points.

YOUNG PEOPLE AS VITAL TO THE FUTURE AND PRESENT OF DEMOCRACY

While children and youth are often discussed in terms of a deficit model owing to their age, they often have a lot to offer to contribute to democracy, and may even draw on their age as a strength, giving them special access and ability that differs from that of adults. When young people do this, their message may spread far and wide, as the image of young people taking strong political stances may disrupt common thinking. I have spoken about Mhairi Black and many young people involved in politics in the three countries I focus on in this book, but I should also note that around the world young people may engage in ways that are both different and similar and reflect diverse experiences of the everyday. For example, Malala Yousafzai, a teenage activist from Pakistan, advocated for girls' education and was shot by the Taliban. For Malala, going to school—which is often seen as an 'everyday' act for many young people in Western democracies—was a critical act of political resistance. She needed to politically resist in seeking to achieve her goal of making school attendance an everyday experience for girls. Speaking at the UN, she called on young people and women, saying '[L]et us pick up our books and pens. They are our most powerful weapons'.[5]

Young people's political engagements can occur in many ways and in a variety of contexts. As quoted in the opening of this chapter, Abby Goldberg, from the United States has said that young people can use their age to their advantage, drawing on their social media skills, friendship circles and free time to get involved and educate busy adults about important problems.[6] Abby certainly has reason to believe in such prospects. At the age of twelve, she became passionate about the problem of plastic bag litter in her home-town and decided to challenge a law proposed in her state legislature that would prevent reduction of plastic bag use. She started an online petition to the governor asking him to veto said legislation, and following a great show of online support the governor did veto the legislation and even rang Abby to thank her for ensuring it was brought to his attention. This case shows how such political successes in the more formal political realm can be achieved through what is often seen as the informal means of young people using social media to share their views and in this case advance a cause of concern to them.

Talking about youth engagement in democracy necessitates thinking about youth participation. In recognising that youth participation is changing while also noting the continued importance of formal politics, I follow Ariadne Vromen's definition for participation: 'acts that can occur, either individually or collectively, that are intrinsically concerned with shaping the society that we want to live in'.[7] Moreover, taking such a broad view of participation is required if I want to understand current youth citizenship practices, since young people are more likely to take part in informal activity than formal politics.[8] Moreover, as Harris, Wyn and Younes have found, just as youth con-tinue to develop individualised, informal strategies for addressing issues that concern them, at the same time many wish for those holding formal political power to listen to their concerns and respond accordingly.[9]

YOUNG PEOPLE, DEMOCRACY AND A STATE POLITICS OF CONCERN

When it comes to citizenship or acting as democrats, both media and govern-ment rhetoric tend to construct young people negatively, suggesting a youth 'problem' in which young people fail to participate politically and exhibit civic-mindedness.[10] Likewise, a state politics of concern is constructed in which governments seek to address the problem, 'fixing' the youth, so they can act as appropriate democratic citizens. Yet such approaches tend to neglect the ways young people are already exhibiting political knowledge and participating in political activity. The issue is not that young people are ignorant or inactive, rather that they are participating less and less in the ways governments would like them to. In short, the common discourse suggests that young people aren't doing politics right and when they do participate it is either not recognised or critiqued for being 'the wrong kind' of participation. Akin to the 'doctor knows best' development model, a government created,

led and controlled approach is most often pursued and delivered by adults to
or at young people, as opposed to with and alongside them—a point I draw
out especially in chapters 1 and 3.

Unfortunately, as Helen Berents so clearly put it, too often 'when young
people engage in politics their actions are deemed illegitimate'.[11] Here I can
consider how young people have responded to austerity measures that will
impact their lives and that of their generation now and in the future, while
also considering media and government responses. For example, in Australia
in 2014 the federal government released budget proposals that would most
harshly affect those already politically marginalised in many ways, disabled
persons, women, unemployed people, students and young people.[12] Many,
including students and youth, responded by taking to the streets in a series
of protests held around the country. At a Melbourne event protesting higher
education cuts, three police officers carried at least one protestor, a fifteen-
year-old girl called Tallulah, away from the scene. The *Herald Sun* newspaper
printed a front-page photo of her removal with the headline 'Hey mum, look
at me', trivialising her very real concern that she and her peers would have
their futures directly affected by the proposed budget cuts they were protesting.[13] Melbourne's Lord Mayor weighed in, saying it was 'inappropriate'
for a 'schoolgirl' to be protesting.[14] Instead, he suggested, it would be more
effective for her to write a polite letter to the Prime Minister expressing her
views.[15] The same day Australia's Prime Minister and Education Minister
scrapped a visit to Deakin University in Melbourne, citing concerns that
students might protest and cause trouble, implying that public protests are
not a 'correct' or 'legitimate' form of political participation.[16] Young people
Tallulah's age are unable to vote, and young people are disallowed from
legitimately taking up space in their preferred ways politically. Yet when they
engage in democratic public protest they are also told they're not doing things
the 'right' way. These limitations and omissions are important to interrogate.
After all, 'if our accounts and understandings of politics miss youth, what
might be missing from our accounts and understandings of politics'?[17]

Governments report a strong interest in young people participating in
democracy—in the ways adult government officials want and expect them to
participate. This tunnel vision ignores young people's reality. Indeed, young
people often face particular political challenges that matter to them, and these
often differ from the main concerns or viewpoints of adults. For example,
a representative survey of young people in Australia found that the top five
issues they would like to see addressed by politicians include: housing affordability and availability, youth unemployment, high costs of tertiary education,
improving the quality of primary and secondary education, and binge drinking
and alcohol-fuelled violence.[18] All of these disproportionately impact young
people and are serious political concerns. Moreover, when Australian surveys

have included both older and younger respondents, young people's priorities differed from others. For example, the majority of young people supported marriage equality, with 45 per cent of them listing it as one of the top five broader community issues politicians ought to address, compared with only 22 per cent of older cohorts. Furthermore, 35 per cent of young people listed gender equality and women's rights among the top five community issues needing political action, compared to only 19 per cent of respondents across older age groups.[19]

Although there is a clear need for governments to engage young people politically, youth tend to remain excluded from formal political processes. At the same time, youth are often portrayed as deficient or future citizens as opposed to valuable current actual and potential contributors to democracy. Indeed, here I suggest that when it comes to young people's engagement with democratic citizenship, the apparent gap or problem is largely constructed by adults and governments themselves, as they exclude young people, fail to listen to them and accept and perpetuate inaccurate, partial visions of the ways young people participate (or don't) politically.

Following the deficit model and the 'state-knows-best' approach, it is commonly further assumed that an appropriate citizenship education will rectify this deficit.[20] However, little investigation has been done to consider whether this assumption actually stacks up to scrutiny.[21] In this book I suggest that traditional civics education is necessary but not sufficient and requires rethinking to move away from the deficit model and towards a more inclusive approach better suited to effectively engaging youth. It is important to note issues with school-based civics education—Derry Hannam has suggested that 'learning about democracy in (an undemocratic) school is like reading holiday brochures in prison'.[22] At the same time, however, there is no need to throw the school out with the deficit water, so to speak. After all, schools are where many young people spend most of their days and can be a site for critical action and education. As one participant in the Australian Youth Affairs Coalition study put it, 'Education is important to me as it illuminates the future, shows the way forward and gives us hope and the ability to tackle any challenges presented to us'.[23] Indeed, statements such as this may offer hope for adults and governments—the development of policies, practices and systems that are more welcoming and responsive to young people will benefit everyone. To move in this direction, it is first important to understand some of the ways many young people already do participate, why and how.

GETTING REAL ABOUT YOUTH PARTICIPATION

Having argued that young people are essential to a healthy democracy, here it is wroth exploring how young people already participate politically in a myriad of ways. Some scholarship on young people and politics tends to differentiate between 'serious' activities and leisure activities, which can significantly influence whether and how we see the political implications of many youth activities that are characterised as leisure pursuits, such as music or theatre-based programmes. For example, Ardizzone suggests that what distinguishes the young people engaged in peacebuilding in her study in the United States is that they sought out action in political, global groups, rather than recreational or social organisations.[24] Although the effect is probably not intended, proposing such dichotomies can bolster ideas of ' "serious" youth vs. "lazy" youth or "real" politics vs. "mere" leisure'.[25]

Here I join with many other scholars who have seen the merit in understanding how political the everyday can be and thus avoid characterising political action as in opposition to recreational or social pursuits. In this way, instead of seeing some youth as the 'good future citizens' who participate in the 'right' ways and others as contrastingly 'apathetic' or 'self-interested', I can work to develop more nuanced, accurate understandings of the diverse ways young people engage with and are impacted by politics in their everyday lives, which represent a range of experiences and approaches. Hence, it is crucial that I better understand the ways youth participate, often in 'everyday' ways, in their schools, communities and online.

As Harris, Wyn and Younes have articulated, the nature of young people's participation has changed towards the everyday in recent times, as life trajectories have become more unpredictable and traditional institutions have become fragmented.[26] International large-scale surveys have indicated a shift towards growing dissatisfaction with the ways democratic processes function and a reduced sense of the relevance of government to the lives of individuals.[27] This has been documented at multiple levels, as most of Harris and Wyn's Australian research participants saw their local government as ineffective and failing to respond well to the needs and interests of youth.[28] Similar results have been documented in the United Kingdom, where youth are demonstrably less likely than older people to indicate an interest in formal politics, affiliate with a political party, vote or indicate extensive political knowledge,[29] and in the United States, where low voter turnout by youth has been seen as cause for concern.[30] More broadly, it is widely accepted that many young people around the world today no longer see state-oriented activism or state-based politics as relevant, and that they no longer gain meaning from the chance to participate or affiliate in traditional ways.[31]

Young people also engage in political participation and learn about and practice citizenship through a variety of creative, informal practices in their everyday lives. This includes activities in their schools and neighbourhoods, and these practices can have a significant impact for the young people involved and their wider communities. It also includes young people's creation of opportunities that connect across difference in the diverse communities in which many live, such as informal, everyday involvement in arts, music, dance and theatre.[32] Through such activities, youth are creating a new mode of civic participation and connectedness.[33]

Unfortunately, many state efforts to involve youth in political participation have focused on the deficit model previously discussed, in which the concerns of youth are not taken seriously and politicians show little interest in their views.[34] Many feel that young people's common dislike for formal politics is not because they are indifferent or lack knowledge, but rather because they are excluded from or disregarded in spaces where politics are debated.[35] Hence, they make a case for space within existing political structures and the language used therein in order to 'bridge the gap between formal and everyday politics'.[36]

At the same time, Vromen notes young people's preference for individualised political action such as donating time and money or boycotting, and thus urges scholars to 'anticipate heterogeneity in young people's approach to political participation'.[37] Likewise, she proposes that accurately understanding youth political participation requires us to take into account the ways they actually experience citizenship at present, including accounting for shifting socioeconomic conditions and structural factors like class, race and gender.[38] Even though youth tend to occupy liminal spaces and be accorded a liminal status, this can in turn give them a unique standpoint towards social issues, enabling them to respond differently to adults.[39] Additionally young people's politics may be frequently influenced by their embeddedness in particular spaces and their relations with adults, in which youth can exhibit both resourcefulness and agency.[40] This includes bridging public/private political divides, such as making friends across cultures,[41] even when the elders in their families may 'stick to their own'.

IN THE MIX WITH YOUTH POLITICS

Although youth tend to dislike and avoid formal, traditional political involvement, the variety of ways young people participate politically in everyday ways are readily apparent. For example, my previous research with youth peacebuilding programmes in Australia and Northern Ireland found that music could be effectively used to engage young people in addressing conflict in their communities through nonviolent means. One peer leader in her twenties, when asked about why she found music a useful tool, noted that '[I]t's easy because people love music if you kind of measure that with just running a peacebuilding workshop without music, I'm not sure if the general public would be actually interested in like if you're gonna create a ten-page document'.[42] Another teen participant in the same programme in Australia remarked that he would have been uninterested in attending a programme with the same aim—peacebuilding—that instead of using music expected the youth participants to 'like sit down in a room and like, talk about peace, like, you know, you go to church on a Sunday'.[43] In this way, these young people illustrate how many youth care about issues and want to be involved in affecting social change in ways that are relevant, interesting, participatory and engaging for them as opposed to more formal, traditional means that may have served past generations but are no longer seen as widely relevant to this one.

Semi-formal Participation

What then are some of the issues young people care about and how do they see themselves working to address them? As previously noted, these issues can include things as wide ranging as environmental concerns—reducing the usage of single-use plastic bags and security concerns—to the right of girls to attend school safely. To consider this more deeply, here I report on some of the ideas generated during a one-day young women's high school leadership forum held in 2012 in a regional centre in Australia.[44] The programme was developed and delivered by volunteer members of a political organisation for young women, all of whom were either enrolled in university or recent graduates and between twenty and thirty years of age. As the organisation was at the time affiliated with the United Nations, this group may be seen as engaged in 'semi-formal' participation, given the links with an international political body. The young women who participated came from several local schools and spent the day exploring issues that mattered to them and ways they aim to contribute to social and political change as leaders now and in the future.

Part of this forum consisted of opening and closing workshops in which participants worked individually and in groups to identify issues of concern for them and map out ways they could be involved in redressing said issues. After some introductory presentations and teambuilding work to form groups, the girls engaged in an activity called 'That's Not On'.[45] Each girl was given a printout of a big grey light bulb, on which she could write down the issue(s) that she found most concerning. They then posted these up on the wall and were able to share and make connections between their issues of concern, which were wide-ranging and included highly localised as well as clearly global issues. For example, concerns were frequently expressed around violence (both at the intimate, local level, e.g. child abuse and sexual abuse and at the international level, e.g. global conflict and war), poverty, bullying, human trafficking, internet safety issues (such as bullying, stalking or fighting via Facebook), racism, inequality (based on gender, race and sexuality), access to quality education, environmental concerns, approaches to dealing with refugees, support for mental health, health systems to prevent and address disease, economic instability, and joblessness.

Following this activity and discussions on why they had chosen the issues they had, participants engaged in several skills station activities and issues workshops, in which they defined the qualities of leader from their point of view, debated different approaches to political participation and practiced critical thinking skills using creative means to consider, for example, how women in leadership roles are often represented. Before wrapping up for the day, the students engaged in a final workshop in which they revisited the issues they had generated at the beginning of the day and worked individually and then in teams to identify one or more issues on which to focus.

They then worked together to create an action plan, focusing on what they could do and how they could do it in terms of redressing the issues they had identified. Some of the actions many proposed taking included raising funds and awareness through assemblies, posters, and/or newsletters. Others also suggested more radical actions, such as protesting women's exclusion from certain areas of the armed forces through hosting a mock funeral or staging a walk out at work to protest gender wage inequality. Creative approaches suggested also included making a music video to share ideas about pursuing gender equality. Some groups came up with very detailed plans for how they could implement their ideas, including addressing questions of why the action would be useful, what resources it would require, how they could be obtained and how they could get others involved.

While it is not possible to make any claims about what they went on to do with these plans, in the evaluation forms students did list several ways they would use the information and skills gathered in the forum, including continuing 'to fundraise for overseas women and youth' and 'explaining to others what happened and give them inspiration to make a difference'. Some also pointed out that what they enjoyed most about the forum was 'talking to other girls and sharing ideas and opinions' and having the 'chance to bring up issues and hear what others think'. As one said, 'The group activities were great because we got to share our ideas and learn more about each other and our schools. Making new friends as well. Speakers were amazing'. In this way, the participant indicates the value she places on having a say herself, being heard by and being able to hear from her peers, and learning from older peers and adults about relevant experience.

Such engagements have much to tell us about what young people do care about and how they are and aspire to be politically active and engaged. In this case, the young people's participation and reports on their own experiences indicate that youth should not be assumed to be apathetic or uninformed even if they've not previously been involved in traditional political participation. Rather, when I ask, I often find out many young people are aware of many political issues and are capable of thinking through ways of addressing them that are relevant to their lives and those of their peers. These approaches often fall in the 'everyday' realm.

Online [Virtual] Participation

The Internet, particularly social media, has been of growing interest to scholars exploring the everyday activities of young people, with research reporting that social media use among youth in 2012 was at 80 per cent in the United States, 90 per cent in Australia and 94 per cent in the United Kingdom.[46] This widespread usage has meant that individual youth no longer need to join formal political organisations in order to take part in or learn about collective political action.[47] This can be especially important for young people who have limited access to actual physical public spaces,[48] such as the young women involved in the Arab Spring movement.[49] Indeed, the online environment, which enables new ways to protest, has created a drastically different generation of activism,[50] given the disproportionate use of social media by younger people.[51]

Some research has also found that online political participation can lead to gains in offline participation.[52] As Xenos, Vromen and Loader found in their study, youth who used social media were also more likely to engage politically in other ways.[53] This was true in the United Kingdom, the United States and in Australia. At the same time, for youth groups engaged in political action, Facebook has become, either reluctantly or enthusiastically, a normal tool for organising.[54] This is unsurprising given that social networking platforms are significant places for youth to link in with their peers, building networks locally and globally.[55] After all, evidence indicates that compared to previous generations, today's youth are more able to utilise the digital political environment to their advantage, as Millennials are more likely to engage in texting (SMS), email and social networking.[56] Hence, while research hasn't shown strong links between social media use and individual engagement, Xenos, Vromen and Loader have found significant support for social media use and collective political engagement.[57]

In a more unspectacular, mundane and everyday sense, the Internet has allowed youth 'to "have a say" . . . and thereby express social and political concerns and share views with others, especially peers'.[58] As Ekstrom observes, on social media 'you read more than you write', so young people 'can follow discussions without being expected to go public with their own voices. They can reflect upon their own opinions and pick up things to discuss with peers in other settings'.[59] At the same time, this will not always be the case, and the likelihood that it will differs among users. As Ekstrom notes, most experience Facebook, for example, as a risky place for dealing with controversial issues,[60] as they fear 'face-threatening responses'. Such responses are a real concern, especially for particular groups of young people, as social media tends to reinforce social equalities. Girls, for example, are especially concerned about risks they can face in this environment in which they face particular vulnerabilities.[61]

Overall, online activity, including social media is clearly important to the way youth do politics, but it should be understood in conjunction with other forms of action rather than seen as the central driving force behind it. Nor should online activity be idealised or over-interpreted as always constituting civic participation or assumed to undo intersecting inequalities.[62] Online does not necessarily equal outsiders coming in. Indeed, little consistent evidence supports the idea that the Internet mobilises more youth into emergent ways of engaging politically.[63] Likewise, the virtual, online spaces youth inhabit must be analysed and understood alongside the local ways they negotiate belonging and develop a sense of community.[64] As Harris articulates, 'The point here is not that young people are constructing community online in ways that either disrupt their capacity to create a strong sense of local identity, or see them renouncing the physical for the virtual'.[65]

MOVING FORWARD ON YOUTH POLITICAL PARTICIPATION WITH THE EVERYDAY IN MIND

While these vignettes reflect more everyday modes of participation, I should not forget or give up on prospects for including and incorporating young people in more formal political ways, including in governmental decision-making. Young people's participation in such ways can and does happen, especially with local government initiatives, which youth often see as more relevant and accessible. Local context matters a great deal to how young people experience and participate in politics, so options for engaging with local government are particularly valuable and can give young people experience in working to have a say and create change from their local communities all the way to the global level. Indeed, young people are often at the nexus of the local and global given the ways they interact and contribute in their neighbourhoods and schools, as well as through online global connectivity. So rather than seeing these as distinct and in some hierarchy of priority, such actions can best be understood on a spectrum or continuum of potential political participation, in which both formal and informal activities can be and are important and relevant.

While on average, young people do tend to dislike or avoid formal, traditional modes of political participation, they are actively involved in many other ways. Indeed, research suggests that the main issues that concern marginalized young people, and likewise the issues on which these young people want to actively participate in decision-making, are mainly those impacting their everyday lives in public space, education and work.[66] Scholars, policymakers and those working with youth can learn from these everyday lived experiences of young people and use that knowledge to respond better, working with youth realities rather than against them. Doing so means working with young people, who often prefer youth-led or youth-controlled activities that are located where young people already are and in which they feel they can make a difference.[67]

Given this, and the cultures of existing schools, it is important that education for democratic citizenship incorporates new directions and alternative and/or supplemental approaches that incorporate an awareness of young people's everyday lives. Research has documented that young people's education for citizenship often occurs in informal ways, such as through their everyday community activities and interactions with their friends, family and the media. Indeed, as Harris and Wyn note, the young people in their studies were most likely to engage politically in 'micro-territories of the local', where they engage in class and with their friends and family around political discussions, and desire more of a say than they already have.[68] Moreover, the literature highlights intersections between macro and micro politics and the related links between different political practices.[69] It is worth remembering that it is the exclusion of young people from traditional formal politics that has led to their creating more informal everyday spaces to practice discussing politics and learning about social and political issues.[70] Furthermore, rethinking civic learning requires moving away from situating any one particular model of citizenship as correct; rather it is crucial to understand citizen identity and reality as dynamic and multiple.[71]

There are, however, examples of youth-oriented activities and organisations that account for complexity and dynamism as they bridge ideas of informal and formal politics and constitute youth as citizens with capacity for positive social change now and in the future. For example, consider the most recent Girl Scout curriculum. Historically, Girl Scouts has consistently aimed to train girls to be resourceful, responsible citizens.[72] In current training efforts, Girl Scouts are tasked with imagining 'a world in which girls could influence policies that really matter—education, health care, housing, employment'.[73] They are also encouraged to create a Take Action Project on a political issue that matters to girls and women and to develop a Global Girls' Bill of Rights. Illustrations for younger girls consistently incorporate racially and ethnically diverse girls and the women and girls profiled exhibit diversity in terms of age, race and ability.[74] Older Girl Scout Seniors also learn about women's rights movements and feminist issues, with intersectionality highlighted to help them develop understandings of collective action and respect for diversity.[75] The training books provided not only encourage girls to look at themselves as leaders, 'they define girls as both current and future leaders', and approach them 'as powerful, and link being powerful with taking action'.[76] Such work is critical since active citizenship necessitates being able to actively take part in social change and establishing active solidarity,[77] which may be possible in both informal and formal ways and both inside and outside the traditional classroom.

Across our experience and research, whether in schools or in their wider communities, young people regularly express a desire for greater application of participatory, active, creative approaches to their involvement.[78] They also want to have fun,[79] challenging the idea that matters of serious consequence must be inherently boring and dealt with as such. Instead, they often believe creative approaches can be used to bring fun to almost any issue or area. Although Vromen and Collin found youth had different ideas on what 'fun' means, it was generally understood as everyday processes promoting entertainment, social interaction, laughter, diverse experiences and a chance for making friends.[80] As with my own previous research with youth programmes,[81] Vromen and Collin's participants also noted that food is a good incentive to attract youth, especially nearly arrived young people, youth from low socio-economic backgrounds and indigenous young people, and youth especially prefer that food be served in ways that facilitate social interaction, as this is seen as fun.[82] Methods of data gathering on young people's views must also take into account this desire for creative, fun approaches, as some youth have said that they discourage youth engagement due to being boring, not seen as 'relevant' due to unclear outcomes, or a lack of practicality in their delivery.

Many youth also noted the ineffectiveness of trying to involve them in surveys, which they saw as 'boring' or 'impractical,' or in formal meetings as a way of getting them active in decision-making.[83] I have also witnessed this in practice. For example, while acting as a volunteer member of a steering for a youth arts organisation, I observed the time period that followed the organisation's decision to appoint two young people to serve on the board. Knowing the two young women, who were heavily involved in the programme and clearly had many good ideas to contribute, it was disappointing to see that they rarely felt free to make suggestions or comments except when directly asked to do so. Noting this, when I was asked to comment I would instead use my speaking time to turn it back to the youth representatives for advice, but this did little to extend their substantive say in the organisation's programming. Likewise, my experience suggests more investigation is needed into more welcoming and effective ways to involve young people in decision-making. As Vromen and Collin note, young people stress that doing so must be informal, flexible and fun and include incentives and spaces and language that are youth friendly.[84]

As noted earlier, schools may often be seen as formal places of traditional methods, but policies and curriculum can be developed to link the formal and the informal and bridge the gap to better ensure relevant, accessible citizenship education for young people, both in and out of school. As Vromen and Collin note, it is worthwhile for policymakers to 'shift their preference for structured, formal participation mechanisms to those which recognize and respond to everyday, local and culturally meaningful forms of participation'.[85] This can and should include student-centred learning for classroom-based citizenship education. When considering school-based learning, a range of recent studies have found the school's level of openness to be important, with specific emphasis on classroom discussion that includes current events and important issues.[86] This might include, for example, city council simulations, which actively engage students in experiential learning on complex issues.[87]

Furthermore, heeding calls for co-designed civics curriculum, which I return to in a later chapter, may offer valuable ways forward, going beyond being open to youth views and needs to actually being centred on them. In any case, new directions must account for enhanced understanding of what constitutes a successful citizenship education, effective ways for understanding young people and the everyday world they inhabit, and attention to diverse approaches that make room for seeing education as action. Nonetheless, as the next section acknowledges, even following such an approach is not without limits, given the current challenges of the global political environment young people inhabit.

CAVEATS AND COMPLICATIONS: THE NEOLIBERAL POLITICAL CONTEXT, INDIVIDUALISATION AND MAKING SPACE FOR DIFFERENCE

Having noted many ways young people can and do engage politically through everyday activities, it is also important to engage with challenges and look at the broader context. Hence, this section discusses caveats and complications to the points previously articulated, with a special interest in the outcomes of neoliberal approaches to political and economic decision-making over the past several decades. Today's youth generation is indeed being disproportionately and negatively affected by the ongoing commitment to neoliberalism in political and economic decision-making. This makes it fairly unsurprising that young people are at the same time becoming more disenchanted with formal, traditional political structures, which have tended to disadvantage their generation. While 'the importance of wealth in modern economies is approaching levels last seen before the First World War',[88] following the Global Financial Crisis (GFC), young people have faced great losses, with their wealth clearly dwindling. Likewise, research suggests that young people today are far less optimistic about their futures than previous generations, and for good reason. Moreover, research reported in the media in the United Kingdom, the United States and Australia, for example, suggests that today's generation of youth have cause for worry, as it does appear they are facing comparatively tough times.

Firstly, consider Australia, where young people today bear the costs of past and present government decision-making,[89] although they have had little say in it. This is despite the fact that young people have always contributed to the budget in a net fashion—working age people pay more taxes than they get in government services and benefits.[90] This will continue as they bear the cost of existing deficits, leaving them with fewer government services, despite the higher taxes they will pay if they are lucky enough to find work. In short, 'Government policy choices have contributed to the size of the future burden on young Australians',[91] while doing little to help them in the here-and-now. Indeed, reports on the Foundation for Young Australians' study suggest that 'Youth today could be the first Australian generation worse-off than their parents', not least because nearly a third of them are under- or unemployed, the majority of their income is spent on housing and they face greater debts for their university education.[92] Similarly, the Grattan Institute's report 'The Wealth of Generations' finds that young Australians of today 'may end up with lower living standards than their parents at the same age'.[93]

A similar situation is reflected in the United States, where the Urban Institute's Opportunity and Ownership Project has found that compared to their parents at the same age, those under thirty are 'worth only half as much', when considering inflation-adjusted wealth.[94] Like in Australia, today's young people in the United States have large and growing university debts, high housing costs and continue to face a tough job market.[95] Likewise, in 2011 only 44 per cent of Americans believed it likely that the youth of today would have a better life than their parents, the lowest number on record since reporting began in 1983.[96]

Studies in the United Kingdom report similar findings. Income gaps between young people and older generations have widened there since the Global Financial Crisis, and people in their twenties suffered the greatest reduction in wealth of all age groups, despite being better qualified than any generation before them, according to the London School of Economics (LSE).[97] LSE research found that 'the economic crisis and its aftermath have not affected everyone equally', with young people faring much worse than their parents.[98] Hence, the researchers concluded that today's young people will see their future wealth determined by intergenerational wealth transfers, which are highly unequally distributed.[99]

This challenging situation for young people is situated within and alongside broader challenges to democracy in our neoliberal times. In November
2014, I attended a public panel on 'Children on Democracy' hosted by the
Wheeler Centre for Books, Writing and Ideas. Panellists included four local
young people from ages eight to thirteen. The panellists were asked about a
variety of topics, including money, power and politics in democracy, and one
thirteen-year-old girl participating noted that

> there is probably corruption in democracy, like people just pay off people not to
> say anything, to just forget about an issue and to kind of like steer away from it
> because they don't want their business to be affected by it. Like, um, if my sister
> told me to go do something for her which maybe was a bit . . . naughty, I would
> probably say no, but if she said I will give you five bucks I would say yeah, sure . . .
> I don't think that is how it should be, because they [business leaders seeking undue
> influence on government] are only thinking about money and they are not thinking
> about everyone else; and I think that if business were in charge of everything that
> was going on in the world, it would be a very sad [money-focused] world and . . .
> I think it would be a much worse place.

While this young woman is using knowledge and examples from her everyday life to understand and explain this political–economic nexus, she demonstrates a high level of analysis in line with several current global debates
and discussions on the links between extreme economic inequality and the
crises this inequality creates in democracies. For example, high-profile
organisations such as Oxfam have made similar claims in global forums.
Oxfam Executive Director Winnie Byanyima emphasises that 'Our current
economic system is not working at many levels'.[100] This system, she says,
overemphasises possible benefits of the market, helps only a narrow range of
elite actors, fails the majority and furthermore fails the planet.[101] Moreover,
Byanyima argues, the current system did not arise accidentally but rather
through deliberate policy choices that resulted from leaders responding to
elite minorities instead of the majority. In doing so, majority rights have been
continuously undercut as a result of such power and wealth disparities.[102] In
short, her views criticising the current political–economic system as bad for
democracies are well in line with that of the thirteen-year-old girl cited above,
as Byanyima argues that

> [E]xtreme inequality is . . . frequently linked to rising restrictions on civic space
> and democratic rights as political and economic elites collude to protect their
> interests. The right to peaceful protest and the ability of citizens to challenge the
> prevailing economic discourse is being curtailed almost everywhere, for elites
> know that extreme inequality and participatory democracy cannot co-exist for
> long.[103]

Another 'Children on Democracy' participant, an eleven-year-old boy, shared similar concerns about democracy as currently practiced around him, noting that

> money is a big part of it, like if you've got a lot of money you sort of find, and that you've got a company or if you're a politician you have more . . . say, because . . . if you've got more money, you are just sort of more in control.

In this way, many children and youth show they are concerned with the way the current political–economic system deals with fairness and 'having a say', and they reflect broader concerns that massive inequality can contribute to weakening those forms of democracy that are predicated on egalitarianism—especially in terms of material wealth and time outside of labour. This goes hand in hand with youth turning away from formal political institutions as the major sites in which they engage with and practice democracy and citizenship.

Global economic restructuring has created significant political changes, leaving individuals with greater personal risk and responsibility.[104] The challenges of economic insecurity have left youth needing to focus on work and study in new ways.[105] This has been noted in the United Kingdom, the United States and Australia, where neoliberal ideologies have played a strong role in 'shaping youth subjectivities primarily around work and consumption'.[106] At the same time, global markets, movements and communications have challenged state-defined citizenship, while individualization, broader neoliberal ideology and job insecurity have alienated youth from formal politics.[107] Thus, as Harris, Wyn and Younes argue, 'it is not surprising that young people's political participation is declining, and scholars argue that disengagement is a logical response to these conditions'.[108]

Given this context of individualisation and youth movement away from formal politics, Vromen asks a critical question: 'What does this mean for social movements and for democracy; and how does it change collective action in general'?[109] While the individualised political practices of young people are often trivialized or given little credit, it is important to note that at the same time, 'young people often choose to work horizontally with their peers, rather than with hierarchical authority, thus their social circles are an important source of information, as well as support'.[110] Likewise the crises in democracies may actually be opening up new spaces and methods for democratic action that include and flow from their everyday lived experiences.

Finally, while the continuation of neoliberal economic and political systems have led to a focus on individualization and thus individuals, youth studies scholars have also highlighted that we cannot forego structural analyses, particularly given the diversity of young people's experience, which is affected greatly by structural factors, and since factors such as 'gender, race, and class continue to shape how young people understand their lives and their relationship with politics'.[111] These different structural factors can also influence whether or how young people can participate politically. As Gordon has found, 'parents' concerns over their children's activism, as well as student strategies to navigate these concerns, were deeply embedded in overlapping gender, race, ethnic, and class contexts'.[112]

For example, it is clear that gendered expectations can affect whether and how young people will engage in political participation, with particular barriers and disincentives having been documented for girls. Harris, Wyn and Younes found that while girls expressed greater concern about political and social issues, and took more political action as broadly understood, at the same time the young women felt 'more excluded from conventional modes of participation'.[113] Likewise, Vromen also found that young women, compared to young men, were more likely to be involved in activism, and thus suggested 'that gender has an important relationship with participatory practice',[114] a point that is also supported by Gordon's work in the United States.[115] This matters not only in formal, conventional modes of participation, but also in more everyday ways that young people may get involved. Research in Australia, for example, has found that when it comes to mainstream cultural activities like sport, which may be part of young people's everyday political engagement, 'young women have far fewer chances than young men to participate in these kind of programs'.[116]

Moreover, research has also concluded that social class differences remain in civic engagement, for youth as well as for adults, and recent changes in youth biographies suggest 'that social inequalities in civic engagement may be growing over time for young people'.[117] Wray-Lake and Hart, for example, found that voting declined over time only for less-educated youth, with recent years seeing increased social inequality in young people's civic engagement.[118,119]

Overall, social, economic and political shifts over the past several decades have seen changes to the ways young people engage in politics. Today's youth are less likely to engage in formal, traditional politics or in the ways that adults would like to participate. However, many young people are politically active in a variety of everyday ways that incorporate activities and knowledge derived from their everyday experiences. While dominant discourses have pushed youth towards individualized approaches to politics in some ways, they have also highlighted remaining structural inequalities. At the same time, youth have shown that while their strategies, often deemed as individualized or trivialized for being too informal or everyday, can actually have significant outcomes, including challenging our notions of what it means to work together democratically. After all, as youth have shown less hierarchical and more networked forms of participation and engagement, they may be showing us a move towards a rethinking of democracy that better accounts for people's everyday lives and the lived experiences of difference.

NOTES

1. Report of the Civics Expert Group (1994). Whereas the people: civics and citizenship education. Canberra: Australian Government Publishing Service.

2. See for example: Marsh, D., T. O'Toole and S. Jones (2006). *Young People and Politics in the UK: Apathy or Alienation.* London: Palgrave Macmillan; Stoker, G. (2006). *Why Politics Matter: Making Democracy Work.* Gordonsville: Palgrave Macmillan; Harris, A. and J. Wyn (2010). 'Guest Editorial Special Issue of YOUNG on "Emerging forms of youth participation: Everyday and local perspectives"'. *Young: Nordic Journal of Youth Research* 18 (1): 3–7; Pruitt, L. J. (2013). *Youth Peacebuilding: Music, Gender & Change.* Albany: State University of New York (SUNY) Press.

3. See for example: Vromen, A. (2003). 'Traversing time and gender: Australian young people's participation'. *Journal of Youth Studies* **6** (3): 277–294; Harris, A. and J. Wyn (2009). 'Young people's politics and the micro-territories of the local'. *Australian Journal of Political Science* **44** (2): 327–344; Harris, A., J. Wyn and S. Younes (2010). 'Beyond apathetic or activist youth: 'Ordinary' young people and contemporary forms of participation'. *Young: Nordic Journal of Youth Research* **18** (1): 9–32; Vromen, A. and P. Collin 'Everyday youth participation? Contrasting views from Australian policymakers and young people'. 97–112; Manning, N. and K. Edwards (2014). 'Does civic education for young people increase political participation? A systematic review'. *Educational Review* **66** (1): 22–45; Xenos, M., A. Vromen and B. D. Loader (2014). 'The great equalizer? Patterns of social media use and youth political engagement in three advanced democracies'. *Information, Communication & Society* **17** (2): 151–167; Vromen, A., M. A. Xenos and B. D. Loader (2015). 'Young people, social media and connective action: from organisational maintenance to everyday political talk'. *Journal of Youth Studies* **18** (1): 80–100.

4. For more on the notion of the 'everyday' in politics, see Bang (2010).

5. Pruitt, L. J. (2014). 'The women, peace and security agenda: Australia and the agency of girls'. *Australian Journal of Political Science* **49** (3): Australian Journal of Political Science. @ 490.

6. LaMotte, D. (2014). *Worldchanging 101: Challenging the Myth of Powerlessness.* Black Mountain, NC: Dryad Publishing. @ 197.

7. Harris, A., J. Wyn and S. Younes (2010). 'Beyond apathetic or activist youth: "Ordinary" young people and contemporary forms of participation'. *Young: Nordic Journal of Youth Research* **18** (1): 9–32. @ 10. [citing Vromen 2003: 82–83]

8. Ibid. @ 22. [citing Smith et al. 2005: 441; Roker 2008, Vromen 2003]

9. Ibid. @ 23.

10. Ibid.

11. Berents, H. (2014). Slackers or delinquents? No, just politically engaged youth. *The Conversation*. Online 4 June 2014.

12. Ibid.

13. Ibid.

14. Ibid.

15. Ibid.

16. Ibid.

17. Ibid.

18. Adair, K. and R. Reodica (2013). *Australia's Youth Matters: Young People Talk About What's Important to Them*. Surry Hills, NSW: Australian Youth Affairs Coalition.

19. Ibid. @ 8–10.

20. For more on this, see Vromen, A. and P. Collin (2010). 'Everyday youth participation? Contrasting views from Australian policymakers and young people'. *Young: Nordic Journal of Youth Research* **18** (1): 97–112. Harris, A. and J. Wyn *ibid*. 'Guest editorial special issue of YOUNG on "Emerging forms of youth participation: Everyday and local perspectives"*. 3–7.

21. Edwards, K. (2007). 'From deficit to disenfranchisement: reframing youth electoral participation'. *Journal of Youth Studies* **10** (5): 539–555; Manning, N. and K. Edwards (2014). 'Does civic education for young people increase political participation? A systematic review'. *Educational Review* **66** (1): 22–45.

22. *Research on democratic schools*, Derry Hannam, www.educationrevolution. org/derhanrep.html

23. Adair, K. and R. Reodica (2013). *Australia's Youth Matters: Young People Talk About What's Important to Them*. Surry Hills, NSW: Australian Youth Affairs Coalition. @ 5.

24. Ardizzone, L. (2003). 'Generating peace: a study of nonformal youth organizations'. *Peace and Change* **28** (3): 420–445.

25. Pruitt, L. J. (2013). *Youth Peacebuilding: Music, Gender & Change*. Albany: State University of New York (SUNY) Press.

26. Harris, A., J. Wyn and S. Younes (2010). 'Beyond apathetic or activist youth: "Ordinary" young people and contemporary forms of participation'. *Young: Nordic Journal of Youth Research* **18** (1): 9–32. @ 9.

27. Bennett, W. L., C. Wells and A. Rank (2009). 'Young citizens and civic learning: two paradigms of citizenship in the digital age'. *Citizenship Studies* **13** (2): 105–120. @ 107. [citing Inglehart 1997]

28. Harris, A. and J. Wyn (2009). 'Young people's politics and the micro-territories of the local' *Australian Journal of Political Science* **44** (2): 327–344. @ 341.

29. Harris, A., J. Wyn and S. Younes (2010). 'Beyond apathetic or activist youth: "Ordinary" young people and contemporary forms of participation'. *Young: Nordic Journal of Youth Research* **18** (1): 9–32. @ 11. [citing Furlong and Carmel 2007]

30. Vromen, A. (2011). 'Constructing Australian Youth Online'. *Information, Communication & Society* **14** (7): 959–980. @ 960 [citing Furlong and Carmel 2007; pp. 21–37]

31. Harris, A., J. Wyn and S. Younes (2010). 'Beyond apathetic or activist youth: "Ordinary" young people and contemporary forms of participation'. *Young: Nordic Journal of Youth Research* **18** (1): 9–32. @ 10.

32. Harris, A. (2013). *Young People and Everyday Multiculturalism.* New York & London: Routledge. @ 112; Pruitt, L. J. (2015). 'Multiculturalism at Play: Young People and Citizenship in Australia'. *Journal of Youth Studies*; Chou, M., J.-P. Gagnon and L. J. Pruitt (2016). 'Putting participation on stage: examining participatory theatre as an alternative site for political participation'.

33. Harris, A. (2013). *Young People and Everyday Multiculturalism.* New York & London: Routledge. @ 112. [citing Vinken 2007:53]

34. Harris, A., J. Wyn and S. Younes (2010). 'Beyond apathetic or activist youth: 'Ordinary' young people and contemporary forms of participation'. *Young: Nordic Journal of Youth Research* **18** (1): 9–32. @ 20.

35. Ibid. @ 21.

36. Ibid.

37. Vromen, A. (2003). 'Traversing time and gender: Australian young people's participation'. *Journal of Youth Studies* **6** (3): 277–294. @ 292.

38. Ibid. @ 277.

39. Wood, B. (2012). 'Crafted within liminal spaces: Young people's everyday politics'. *Political Geography* **31** (2012): 337–346. @ 337.

40. Ibid.

41. Ibid. @ 341.

42. Pruitt, L. J. (2013). *Youth Peacebuilding: Music, Gender & Change.* Albany: State University of New York (SUNY) Press. @ 88–89.

43. Ibid. @ 69.

44. Pruitt, L. J. (2014). 'The women, peace and security agenda: Australia and the agency of girls'. *Australian Journal of Political Science* **49** (3): Australian Journal of Political Science. @ 490.

45. A colloquial phase in Australian English, meaning something that is not right or fair.

46. Vromen, A., M. A. Xenos and B. D. Loader (2015). 'Young people, social media and connective action: from organisational maintenance to everyday political talk'. *Journal of Youth Studies* **18** (1): 80–100. @ 83. [citing Pew Research 2012 and Essential Media Report 2012]

47. Ibid. @ 83.

48. Harris, A. (2013). *Young People and Everyday Multiculturalism.* New York & London: Routledge. @ 109. [citing Boyd 2007:14]

49. For more on this see: Pruitt, L. J. (2014). 'The women, peace and security agenda: Australia and the agency of girls'. *Australian Journal of Political Science* **49** (3): Australian Journal of Political Science.

50. Harris, A., J. Wyn and S. Younes (2010). 'Beyond apathetic or activist youth: "Ordinary" young people and contemporary forms of participation'. *Young: Nordic Journal of Youth Research* **18** (1): 9–32. @ 26.

51. Xenos, M., A. Vromen and B. D. Loader (2014). 'The great equalizer? Patterns of social media use and youth political engagement in three advanced democracies'. *Information, Communication & Society* **17** (2): 151–167. @ 153.

52. Garcia-Castanon, M., A. D. Rank and M. A. Barreto (2011). 'Plugged In or Tuned Out? Youth, Race, and Internet Usage in the 2008 Election'. *Journal of Political Marketing* **10**: 115–138. @ 115.

53. Xenos, M., A. Vromen and B. D. Loader (2014). 'The great equalizer? Patterns of social media use and youth political engagement in three advanced democracies'. *Information, Communication & Society* 17 (2): 151–167. @ 151.

54. Vromen, A., M. A. Xenos and B. D. Loader (2015). 'Young people, social media and connective action: from organisational maintenance to everyday political talk'. *Journal of Youth Studies* **18** (1): 80–100. @ 90.

55. Harris, A. (2013). *Young People and Everyday Multiculturalism.* New York & London: Routledge. @ 108.

56. Garcia-Castanon, M., A. D. Rank and M. A. Barreto (2011). 'Plugged in or tuned out? Youth, race, and internet usage in the 2008 election'. *Journal of Political Marketing* **10**: 115–138. @ 118.

57. Xenos, M., A. Vromen and B. D. Loader (2014). 'The great equalizer? Patterns of social media use and youth political engagement in three advanced democracies'. *Information, Communication & Society* **17** (2): 151–167. @ 161.

58. Harris, A., J. Wyn and S. Younes (2010). 'Beyond apathetic or activist youth: "Ordinary" young people and contemporary forms of participation'. *Young: Nordic Journal of Youth Research* **18** (1): 9–32. @ 26.

59. Ekstrom, M. (2015). 'Young people's everyday political talk: a social achievement of democratic engagement'. *Journal of Youth Studies.* @ 13.

60. Ibid. @ 14; 1.

61. Ibid. @ 17 [citing Boyd 2014: 160; Abiala and Hernwall 2013; Livingstone et al. 2014]

62. Harris, A. (2013). *Young People and Everyday Multiculturalism.* New York & London: Routledge.

63. Vromen, A., M. A. Xenos and B. D. Loader (2015). 'Young people, social media and connective action: from organisational maintenance to everyday political talk'. *Journal of Youth Studies* **18** (1): 80–100. @ 82.

64. Harris, A. (2013). *Young People and Everyday Multiculturalism.* New York & London: Routledge. @ 109.

65. Ibid. @ 109–110.

66. Vromen, A. and P. Collin (2010). 'Everyday youth participation? Contrasting views from Australian policymakers and young people'. *Young: Nordic Journal of Youth Research* **18** (1): 97–112. @ 105.

67. Vromen, A. (2011). 'Constructing Australian Youth Online'. *Information, Communication & Society* **14** (7): 959–980. @ 962. [citing Montgomery et al. 2004 pp. 17–18]; Vromen, A. and P. Collin (2010). 'Everyday youth participation? Contrasting views from Australian policymakers and young people'. *Young: Nordic Journal of Youth Research* **18** (1): 97–112. @ 104.

68. Harris, A. and J. Wyn (2009). 'Young people's politics and the micro-territories of the local'. *Australian Journal of Political Science* **44** (2): 327–344. @ 337; 335 [citing Land 2003, 12]; 338.

69. Azmi, F., C. Brun and R. Lund (2013). 'Young people's everyday politics in post-conflict Sri Lanka'. *Space and Polity* **17** (1): 106–122. @ 110.

70. Harris, A. and J. Wyn (2009). 'Young people's politics and the micro-territories of the local'. *Australian Journal of Political Science* **44** (2): 327–344. @ 329.

71. Bennett, W. L., C. Wells and A. Rank (2009). 'Young citizens and civic learning: two paradigms of citizenship in the digital age'. *Citizenship Studies* **13** (2): 105–120. @ 113.

72. High-Pippert, A. (2015). 'Girltopia: girl scouts and the leadership development of girls'. *Girlhood Studies* **8** (2): 137–152. @ 137.

73. Ibid. @ 145. [citing Glick and Shaw 2008:3)

74. Ibid. @ 147.

75. Ibid.

76. Ibid. @ 148.

77. Ross, A. (2007). 'Multiple identities and education for active citizenship'. *British Journal of Educational Studies* **55** (3): 286–303.

78. See for example: Pruitt, L. J. (2013). *Youth Peacebuilding: Music, Gender & Change.* Albany: State University of New York (SUNY) Press; Pruitt, L. J. (2011). 'Music, youth, and peacebuilding in Northern Ireland'. *Global Change, Peace & Security* **23** (2): 207–222; Vromen, A. and P. Collin (2010). 'Everyday youth participation? Contrasting views from Australian policymakers and young people'. *Young: Nordic Journal of Youth Research* **18** (1): 97–112.

79. Vromen, A. and P. Collin (2010). 'Everyday youth participation? Contrasting views from Australian policymakers and young people'. *Young: Nordic Journal of Youth Research* **18** (1): 97–112. @ 105.

80. Ibid. @ 107.

81. Pruitt, L. J. (2013). *Youth Peacebuilding: Music, Gender & Change.* Albany: State University of New York (SUNY) Press.

82. Vromen, A. and P. Collin (2010). 'Everyday youth participation? Contrasting views from Australian policymakers and young people'. *Young: Nordic Journal of Youth Research* **18** (1): 97–112. @ 107.

83. Ibid. @ 108.

84. Ibid.

85. Ibid. @ 109.

86. Bennett, W. L., C. Wells and A. Rank (2009). 'Young citizens and civic learning: two paradigms of citizenship in the digital age'. *Citizenship Studies* **13** (2): 105–120. @ 109. [citing Kahne and Middaugh 2008; Torney-Purta 2002, Gibson and Levine 2003, Campbell 2005, McIntosh et al. 2007, Pasek et al. 2008; Gibson and Levine 2003, McDevitt et al. 2003, Parker 2003, Syvertsen et al. 2007]

87. Rinfret, S. R. (2012). 'Simulating city councils'. *PS: Political Science & Politics* **45** (3): 513–515.

88. Editorial (2014). Thomas Piketty's 'Capital', summarised in four paragraphs. *The Economist.* Online 4 May 2014.

89. Wood, D. and J. Daley (2014). Young Australians Set to Pay for Government Policy Mistakes. *The Conversation.* online.

90. Ibid.

91. Ibid.

92. Owen, J. (2014). Youth Today Could Be the First Australian Generation Worse-off than Parents. *ABC News.* Online

93. Wood, D. and J. Daley (2014). Young Australians Set to Pay for Government Policy Mistakes. *The Conversation.* online.

94. Woodruff, M. (2013). Younger Generations Are Officially Worse Off Today than Their Parents Were. *Business Insider Australia.* Online. 16 March 2013.

95. Ibid.

96. Mendes, E. (2011). *In U.S., Optimism about Future for Youth Reaches All-Time Low. Gallup.* Online.

97. RT News (2015). 'Disunited Kingdom': Educated Youth Worse Off Than Parents' Generation—study. *RT News.* Online.

98. Ibid.

99. Ibid.

100. Winnie Byanyima (2016). 'Our struggles for a better world are all threatened by the inequality crisis'. *HuffPost World Economic Forum* http://www.huffington-post.com/winnie-byanyima/our-struggles-for-a-bette_b_9026582.html Accessed 25 January 2016 2016. [emphasis in the original]

101. Ibid.

102. Ibid.

103. Ibid.

104. Bennett, W. L., C. Wells and A. Rank (2009). 'Young citizens and civic learning: two paradigms of citizenship in the digital age'. *Citizenship Studies* **13** (2): 105–120. @ 106. [citing Beck 1999, 2000]

105. Harris, A., J. Wyn and S. Younes (2010). 'Beyond apathetic or activist youth: "Ordinary" young people and contemporary forms of participation'. *Young: Nordic Journal of Youth Research* **18** (1): 9–32. @ 12. [citing Andres and Wyn, 2010; Lagos and Rose, 1999]

106. Harris, A. and J. Wyn. 'Guest Editorial Special issue of YOUNG on "Emerging forms of youth participation: everyday and local perspectives"'. *Young* **18** (1): 3–7. @ 5.

107. Harris, A., J. Wyn and S. Younes. *'Beyond apathetic or activist youth: "Ordinary" young people and contemporary forms of participation'. Young* **18** (1): 9–32. @ 12. [citing Bauman, 2001; Beck and Beck-Gernsheim, 2001; Giddens, 1992; Faulks, 2000; Furlong and Cartmel, 2007)

108. Ibid. @ 12.

109. Vromen, A. (2011). 'Constructing Australian Youth Online'. *Information, Communication & Society* **14** (7): 959–980. @ 977.

110. Vromen, A., M. A. Xenos and B. D. Loader (2015). 'Young People, Social Media and Connective Action: From Organisational Maintenance to Everyday Political Talk'. *Journal of Youth Studies* **18** (1): 80–100. @ 82. [citing Bennett, Wells, and Freelon 2009, 29]

111. Vromen, A. (2011). 'Constructing Australian Youth Online'. *Information, Communication & Society* **14** (7): 959–980. @ 976. [citing Marsh et al. 2007]

112. Gordon, H. R. (2008). 'Gendered paths to teenage political participation: parental power, civic mobility, and youth activism'. *Gender & Society* **22** (1): 31–55. @ 38.

113. Harris, A., J. Wyn and S. Younes (2010). 'Beyond apathetic or activist youth: "Ordinary" young people and contemporary forms of participation'. *Young: Nordic Journal of Youth Research* **18** (1): 9–32. @ 28.

114. Vromen, A. (2003). 'Traversing time and gender: Australian young people's participation'. *Journal of Youth Studies* **6** (3): 277–294. @ 284.

115. Gordon, H. R. (2008). 'Gendered paths to teenage political participation: parental power, civic mobility, and youth activism'. *Gender & Society* **22** (1): 31–55.

116. Harris, A. (2013). *Young People and Everyday Multiculturalism.* New York & London: Routledge. @ 57.

117. Wray-Lake, L. and D. Hart (2012). 'Growing social inequalities in youth civic engagement'. *PS: Political Science & Politics* **45** (3): 456–461. @ 456.

118. Ibid. @ 456. [citing Finlay, Wray-Lake, and Flanagan 2000]

119. Ibid. @ 459.

REFERENCES

Adair, K. and R. Reodica (2013). *Australia's Youth Matters: Young People Talk About What's Important to Them.* Surry Hills, NSW: Australian Youth Affairs Coalition.

Ardizzone, L. (2003). 'Generating Peace: A Study of Nonformal Youth Organizations'. *Peace and Change* **28** (3): 420–445.

Azmi, F., C. Brun and R. Lund (2013). 'Young People's Everyday Politics in Post-conflict Sri Lanka'. *Space and Polity* **17** (1): 106–122.

Bennett, W. L., C. Wells and A. Rank (2009). 'Young Citizens and Civic Learning: Two Paradigms of Citizenship in the Digital Age'. *Citizenship Studies* **13** (2): 105–120.

Berents, H. (2014). Slackers or Delinquents? No, Just Politically Engaged Youth. *The Conversation.* Online. 4 June 2014.

Bessant, J., R. Farthing and R. Watts (2015). 'Co-designing a Civics Curriculum: Young People, Democratic Deficit and Political Renewal in the EU'. *Journal of Curriculum Studies.*

Chou, M., J.-P. Gagnon and L. J. Pruitt (2016). 'Putting Participation on Stage: Examining Participatory Theatre as an Alternative Site for Political Participation'. *Policy Studies* **36**(6): 607–622.

Editorial (2014). Thomas Piketty's 'Capital', Summarised in Four Paragraphs. *The Economist.* Online. 4 May 2014.

Edwards, K. (2007). 'From Deficit to Disenfranchisement: Reframing Youth Electoral Participation'. *Journal of Youth Studies* **10** (5): 539–555.

Ekstrom, M. (2015). 'Young People's Everyday Political Talk: A Social Achievement of Democratic Engagement'. *Journal of Youth Studies.*

Garcia-Castanon, M., A. D. Rank and M. A. Barreto (2011). 'Plugged In or Tuned Out? Youth, Race, and Interet Usage in the 2008 Election'. *Journal of Political Marketing* **10**: 115–138.

Gordon, H. R. (2008). 'Gendered Paths to Teenage Political Participation: Parental Power, Civic Mobility, and Youth Activism'. *Gender & Society* **22** (1): 31–55.

Harris, A. (2013). *Young People and Everyday Multiculturalism.* New York & London: Routledge.

Harris, A. and J. Wyn (2009). 'Young People's Politics and the Micro-Territories of the Local'. *Australian Journal of Political Science* **44** (2): 327–344.

Harris, A. and J. Wyn (2010). 'Guest Editorial Special issue of YOUNG on 'Emerging Forms of Youth Participation: Everyday and Local Perspectives''. *Young: Nordic Journal of Youth Research* **18** (1): 3–7.

Harris, A., J. Wyn and S. Younes (2010). 'Beyond Apathetic or Activist Youth: "Ordinary" Young People and Contemporary Forms of Participation'. *Young: Nordic Journal of Youth Research* **18** (1): 9–32.

High-Pippert, A. (2015). 'Girltopia: Girl Scouts and the Leadership Development of Girls'. *Girlhood Studies* **8** (2): 137–152.

LaMotte, D. (2014). *Worldchanging 101: Challenging the Myth of Powerlessness.* Black Mountain, NC: Dryad Publishing.

Manning, N. and K. Edwards (2014). 'Does Civic Education for Young People Increase Political Participation? A Systematic Review'. *Educational Review* **66** (1): 22–45.

Marsh, D., T. O'Toole and S. Jones (2006). *Young People and Politics in the UK: Apathy or Alienation.* London: Palgrave Macmillan.

Mendes, E. (2011). In *U.S., Optimism about Future for Youth Reaches All-Time Low. Gallup.* Online.

Owen, J. (2014). Youth Today Could Be the First Australian Generation Worse-off than Parents. *ABC News.* Online

Pruitt, L. J. (2011). 'Music, Youth, and Peacebuilding in Northern Ireland'. *Global Change, Peace & Security* **23** (2): 207–222.

Pruitt, L. J. (2013). *Youth Peacebuilding: Music, Gender & Change.* Albany, State University of New York (SUNY) Press.

Pruitt, L. J. (2014). 'The Women, Peace and Security Agenda: Australia and the Agency of Girls'. *Australian Journal of Political Science* 49(3): Australian Journal of Political Science.

Pruitt, L. J. (2015). 'Multiculturalism at Play: Young People and Citizenship in Australia'. *Journal of Youth Studies.*

Report of the Civics Expert Group (1994). Whereas the People: Civics and Citizenship Education. Canberra, Australian Government Publishing Service.

Rinfret, S. R. (2012). 'Simulating City Councils'. *PS: Political Science & Politics* **45** (3): 513–515.

Ross, A. (2007). 'Multiple Identities and Education for Active Citizenship'. *British Journal of Educational Studies* **55** (3): 286–303.

RT News (2015). 'Disunited Kingdom': Educated Youth Worse-off than Parents' Genderation—Study. *RT News.* Online.

Stoker, G. (2006). *Why Politics Matter: Making Democracy Work.* Gordonsville, Palgrave Macmillan.

Vromen, A. (2003). 'Traversing Time and Gender: Australian Young People's Participation'. *Journal of Youth Studies* 6(3): 277–294.

Vromen, A. (2011). 'Constructing Australian Youth Online'. *Information, Communication & Society* **14** (7): 959–980.

Vromen, A. and P. Collin (2010). 'Everyday Youth Participation? Contrasting Views from Australian Policymakers and Young People'. *Young: Nordic Journal of Youth Research* **18** (1): 97–112.

Vromen, A., M. A. Xenos and B. D. Loader (2015). 'Young People, Social Media and Connective Action: From Organisational Maintenance to Everyday Political Talk'. *Journal of Youth Studies* **18** (1): 80–100.

Winnie Byanyima (2016). 'Our Struggles for a Better World Are All Threatened by the Inequality Crisis'. *HuffPost World Economic Forum http://www.huffington-post.com/winnie-byanyima/our-struggles-for-a-bette_b_9026582.html* Accessed 25 January 2016 2016.

Wood, B. (2012). 'Crafted Within Liminal Spaces: Young People's Everyday Politics'. *Political Geography* **31** (2012): 337–346.

Wood, D. and J. Daley (2014). Young Australians Set to Pay for Government Policy Mistakes. *The Conversation*. online.

Woodruff, M. (2013). Younger Generations Are Officially Worse Off Today than Their Parents Were. *Business Insider Australia*. Online. 16 March 2013.

Wray-Lake, L. and D. Hart (2012). 'Growing Social Inequalities in Youth Civic Engagement'. *PS: Political Science & Politics* **45** (3): 456–461.

Xenos, M., A. Vromen and B. D. Loader (2014). 'The Great Equalizer? Patterns of Social Media Use and Youth Political Engagement in Three Advanced Democracies'. *Information, Communication & Society* **17** (2): 151–167.

Chapter Five

Brexit, Bono and the Entrepreneurial Self

Young People's Participation as 'Global Citizens'

Catherine Hartung and Lesley J. Pruitt

The previous chapters have highlighted the ways in which interest in young people as responsible democratic citizens has grown exponentially since the turn of the century, led by increasingly diverse networks of government, education, business and community sectors. The development of these networks can be understood as part of the patterns of globalisation, which have generated an intensification of politics on a global scale. Consequently, while the previous chapters have focused on young people's political participation domestically—from voting in state elections and joining school councils to participating in community development and public protest—this chapter extends this discussion to consider how the global political landscape positions and critiques young people as 'global citizens'. As within the domestic sphere, in the global context young people are often positioned as either the *problem* or the *solution*. Here we critically engage with the limits of relying on such simplified and stereotypical discourses. In order to understand how complex global discourses construct young people in these ways, and in keeping with the focus on the regions of this book, we consider recent examples from the United Kingdom, the United States, Oxford, and Australia.

First we focus on an example of young people in the United Kingdom being constructed as a problem for failing to take responsibility as global citizens in the case of the 2016 European Union (EU) Referendum, popularly referred to as Brexit. We then look at a case where young people are constructed as a solution to the world's problems through consumption and their accruing 'points' that can be redeemed for tickets to a music festival in New York, championed by transnational celebrity activists such as Bono and Coldplay. We then examine how dominant approaches to global citizenship are articulated in promotional material for Foundation for Young Australians (FYA), an Australian NGO, that positions young people as global entrepreneurs. Through the latter two cases, we explain how discourses situating youth as 'solutions' are often deeply tied to neoliberal approaches.

In critically examining these dominant approaches to youth and global citizenship, we uncover limitations and contend that a more critical and theoretically robust understanding of global citizenship is needed to recognise the complex ways in which young people participate and are seen to participate as 'good' global citizens. We contend that doing so necessarily requires engaging with and critiquing neoliberal discourse as the dominant underlying framework for these constructions of youth. However, in order to engage in these phases of the analysis it is important to consider how global citizenship is commonly understood and analysed.

UNDERSTANDING GLOBAL CITIZENSHIP

The notion of global citizenship derives from the Ancient Greek 'cosmopolitan' (from *kosmopolitês*) or 'citizen of the world'.[1] In more recent and uncertain times, global citizenship has gained popularity with those seeking hopeful and unifying political action. For example, it has been labelled the 'great white hope' of international relations and a 'counterbalance' to political and economic threats.[2] Within this cosmopolitan paradigm of global citizenship, citizens of the world are expected to recognise themselves as members of a global community with shared human interests that go beyond state borders. Likewise, UNESCO's Education Programme (2014–2017) defines global citizenship education as arming young people with knowledge, skills and values founded in 'respect for human rights, social justice, diversity, gender equality and environmental sustainability that empowers learners to be responsible global citizens', allowing young people to recognise their rights and responsibilities 'to promote a better world and future for all'.[3]

It is perhaps not surprising that UNESCO's view of global citizenship and young people's rights is so often cited amongst educators, academics, politicians, policy-makers, the media and various other authorities or sites of authority. Such a view provides a powerful counterpoint to potentially damaging deficit models of young people, which justify young people's exclusion based on their presumed vulnerability, immaturity, incompetence, rebelliousness or incompleteness. In contrast, positioning and educating young people as responsible global citizens provides a more hopeful or optimistic view underpinned by intentions to ensure youth have a voice in political and social spaces from which traditionally they have been excluded. Likewise, UNESCO's model as applied to young people can situate them as a/the solution, in stark contrast to deficit models positioning young people inherently as failures.

The notion of young people as a citizenry of global problem-solvers has garnered support across a range of academic fields, including those engaging with or focusing on children's rights,[4] children's participation[5] and the sociology of childhood.[6] The notion not only positions young people as responsible for making decisions about their day-to-day lives, but as responsible for solving issues of political, social and environmental nature at a national and global scale. In other words, as Stasiulis states, through the global citizenship lens, 'Rather than viewing children as "pre-citizens", or as silent, invisible, passive objects of parental and/or state control and thus justifiably excluded from many civil and political citizenship rights, children are cast as full human beings, invested with agency, integrity, and decision-making capacities'.[7] Take, for instance, Article 1 from the *Convention on the Rights of the Child.* It states that 'a child means every human being below the age of eighteen years unless under the law applicable to the child, majority is attained earlier'. There is too the line from the *Universal Declaration of Human Rights* that every person's childhood is entitled to 'special care and assistance'. Taken together, the care ethic for a child's parent or legal guardian is to do everything in their power to ensure this child with agency, integrity, decision-making capacities and rights can exercise their citizenship as part of 'the full and harmonious development' of their personality 'in an atmosphere of happiness, love and understanding'. This is a view of a full citizen at birth, who must be given a safe space to grow as a human being and to exercise their political agency as they grow—quite a contrast to the pre-citizen view.

A significant body of academic literature advocates for a model of young people as global.[8] This literature focuses on identifying select attributes and behaviours of an ideal global citizen, namely, a citizen who is responsible, empathetic and interculturally aware.[9] By focusing on ideal personal attributes, such literature can present a normative vision, one that privileges certain kinds of young people over others. This can also overlook contextual complexities, particularly the underlying mechanisms that have the power to decide who or what a good global citizen is.

How young people are constituted as good global citizens is strongly tied to wider societal demands that call for global unity while also requiring economic competitiveness and productivity. So, while significant consensus exists among business, scientific and education leaders about the need for creating multidimensional citizens through a curriculum that focuses on worldwide ethical concerns,[10] approaches to educating youth 'carry within them imagined paths to global competitiveness'.[11]

Relating to a whole gamut of environmental, economic and equity problems, from climate change and poverty to human rights abuses, this push has been fuelled by a perceived need to shape the global education of young people around particular human characteristics and responsibilities that are constructed as necessary in an economically interconnected global world. In this context, attention is needed to 'what kind of future globalizations we will tolerate or create, and the social spaces and infrastructures we develop, who is included or excluded—and how'.[12] Support for this normative vision of the young person as the good global citizen is evident beyond academic literature in the work of various transnational celebrity activists and international corporations that fund campaigns and publish materials focused on the promotion of responsible global citizenship.[13]

Here we suggest that the dominant notion of 'good' global citizenship for young people has been strongly shaped by a hegemonic neoliberal discourse of global relations. This neoliberal discourse has grown in prominence since the late 1970s and tends to signify a global economic system in which market-based approaches are prioritized. Following endorsements by powerful actors such as the World Bank and the International Monetary Fund, this doctrine has been emphasised as ' "neutral" best practice', with culture and politics seen as separate from economics.[14] Likewise neoliberal discourse is used here to refer to the corollary hegemonic political discourse, which constructs the world as guided by principles of privatisation, individualisation, freedom and choice.[15] Likewise, inequality is rendered personal, and a key assumption is that there exists an 'equal playing field in which individual actors can and should take responsibility for securing their own positive outcomes' through solving any possible problems through the free market. In this way, neoliberalism overlooks or rejects efforts to address structural inequalities, such as those relating to race, class or gender, despite clear indications that policy approaches grounded in neoliberalism have disproportionately impacted certain groups, such as women,[16] ethnic minorities,[17] and the young.[18]

We suggest that the tendency to emphasise and promote individual responsibility of young people as a means of finding solutions to global problems strongly relates to this neoliberal discourse. More specifically, individual young people are called upon to contribute by enriching themselves or participating in what can be conceptualised as 'selfie humanitarianism'. Koffman, Orgad and Gill use this term to highlight situations where solidarity is expressed through a 'refashioning of the self' based on consumption and processes of self-broadcasting, self-branding and self-promotion.[19] For example, Koffman and Gill[20] in their discussion of the UN Foundation's Girl Up movement, which aims to engage American girls in issues affecting girls of the Global South, describe how American girls are called upon to buy Girl Up products and post pictures online of them wearing the products; as such Girl Up is 'promoted as identity work that will benefit U.S. girls directly—as well as those girls in the Global South'.[21] As Berents points out, such constructions can have significant material implications for young people's everyday lives. After all, as she notes, deploying such 'notions of girlhood as a lens for our engagement in crises in other parts of the globe requires critical consideration as to how to, or even whether we can, avoid problematic narratives of girlhood that obfuscate the complexity of girls' lived experiences'.[22] While these examples focus specifically on girls they indicate how such narrow lenses when applied to youth more broadly can also bring about challenges.

Overall, this discourse of global citizenship functions as a technology of subjection or 'an attempt at a remoralisation of young people',[23] one that produces an 'entrepreneurial self'[24] compatible with dominant neoliberal discourses and ignoring existing inequalities. It is likewise important to explore how, within this framework, young people are simultaneously positioned as failing and as the solution to global politics, with the aim of challenging readers to think beyond such simplistic portrayals and to recognize the agendas underlying them.

In this context of calls for young people's participation as responsible, entrepreneurial actors engaging in self-help, youth are positioned within neoliberal processes and discourses. They are likewise positioned as responsible for governing themselves, a process often referred to as 'responsibilisation'. It is through such regulatory processes that the modern subject is produced and reproduced; an increasing emphasis on self-determination and active citizenship is used to ensure realms outside the state (i.e., the social, private, market and civil society) 'function to the benefit of the nation as a whole'.[25] This neoliberal rationality seeks to achieve congruence between a 'responsible and moral individual' and an 'economic-rational actor'.[26] Through these neoliberal processes of responsibilisation, young people compelled to carefully manage the risks of their own 'DIY project of the Self',[27] a sort of institutionally determined autonomy.

Within this current context of neoliberal globalisation and the conceptions of global citizenship it has generated and sustained, we believe it is important to ask: what are the ways in which young people are positioned as global citizens and how are they evaluated against these standards? We explore these questions through considering recent examples from the United Kingdom, the United States, Oxford, and Australia that reflect common approaches to engaging with youth and global citizenship. The purpose of analysing these examples is not to judge whether they are 'good' or 'bad'. Rather, we are interested in identifying the messages that underpin the texts and the effects these have on how young people are constituted as global citizens.

YOUNG PEOPLE AS 'FAILING' GLOBAL CITIZENS: THE
UNITED KINGDOM'S BREXIT CATASTROPHE

This first section explores how young people were constructed as failing to participate in the European Union (EU) referendum held to decide whether the United Kingdom should exit from the EU. Following several years of mounting pressure from the public concerning Britain's relationship with Europe, the conservative government at the time, led by the then Prime Minister David Cameron, initiated plans for a referendum. Several months of campaigning for both sides ensued and the referendum took place on 23 June 2016. The next morning it was declared that the United Kingdom would leave the EU, with 52 per cent of Brits (who voted) voting to leave, only 4 per cent more than those voting to remain (48 per cent).[28]

The result was greeted with shock and outcry from many U.K. residents and those within Europe more broadly, with much of the concern focusing on economic outcomes and limits to global mobility seen as necessary for economic competitiveness. Cameron then stood down as Prime Minister and was replaced by former Home Secretary Theresa May, who stated during her candidacy speech: 'The campaign was fought . . . and the public gave their verdict. There must be no attempts to remain inside the EU . . . and no second referendum . . . Brexit means Brexit'.[29] This was despite several million Brits having signed a petition calling for a second referendum given the close vote and evidence that many had not understood what they were voting for before the results. In the media aftermath, some commentators focussed on the apparent ignorance of voters, highlighting the soar in people googling questions such as 'What is the EU?' and 'What happens if we leave the EU?' in the hours after voting closed.[30] Other commentators believed the outcome exposed the United Kingdom's racist underbelly and a resistance towards a culturally diverse and globally interconnected society.[31]

A number of studies further analysing voting data from the referendum were released, with reports breaking down the results based on demographic factors such as age. One such report from Sky Data received significant media attention, as they suggested that only 36 per cent of eighteen to twenty-four-year-olds and 58 per cent of twenty-five to thirty-four-year-olds voted in the referendum. Of those who did vote, it was claimed that 75 per cent of eighteen to twenty-four-year-olds voted to remain in the EU.[32] However, further academic analysis suggested previous reports had dramatically underestimated young people's participation. Following post-referendum polling among 2,002 people the results found that 64 per cent of those under twenty-five who were registered did vote, almost twice the estimate provided by Sky Data.[33]

One reason the question about whether or not young people voted is important is that they are arguably the demographic who will be most affected by the decision. After all, while older people had been the deciding vote to leave; they have far less time to live with the consequences compared to young people. Indeed, the criticism directed at young people also failed to acknowledge that many were deemed too young to vote on the issue, even though it will affect them greatly. As one young woman only slightly too young to vote put it:

> One thing that upsets me most is that this decision has been made by people who will not have to live with the consequences for as long as us. Young people voted to remain and older people voted to leave. I feel that I have been let down by an older generation who won't be affected by the volatility of this decision.[34]

Young people who felt similarly expressed their feelings of betrayal and doubt in various ways, including taking to social media with the hashtag #NotInMyName.[35] Tweets, using this hashtag, in the days following the vote (held on 23 June 2016) include a French journalist photographing a young protestor in the United Kingdom with the headline: 'Young people express their rage'; a young postgraduate student writing '#Brexit fallout has simply led to more hatred. If you see it, stand against it. This is not what Britain should become'; and a Tweet from the German news provider Die Welt showing young people protesting the Brexit result. This reaction suggests that this was a case of older generations voting to leave when a strong majority of younger generations wanted to stay.

Yet despite many young people advocating to remain and criticising the outcome of the referendum, it was young people who were often blamed as responsible for the vote resulting in a decision to leave the European Union. Had more young people voted, it was declared, the United Kingdom could have been 'saved' from its fate. At times this critique even came from fellow young people. For example, in an opinion piece titled 'Young people are so bad at voting—I'm disappointed in my peers', Hannah Jane Parkinson expresses her dismay at the lack of action among young people who failed to show up on polling day.[36] While Parkinson acknowledges that there is little certainty regarding demographic turnouts, as there was no exit poll, she maintains that 'nobody can quibble with the assertion that young people in the United Kingdom are bad at voting'. Parkinson directed much of her anger towards what she sees as the most 'infuriating type' of young person—those who are politically engaged but still fail to vote. Parkinson pointed the finger at young people's use of social media, arguing, 'I see that changing your profile picture to a French flag, or a Rainbow flag helps you to feel better and does contribute to a nicer, supportive tone of discourse—it has its place—but when it comes to affecting policy change, it's as good as hovering a pencil over the box and crossing the air'.

In similar opinion pieces, Brexit was declared 'a harsh political awakening for young people',[37] and young people were painted as having little right to be concerned by the outcome. The overarching critique of such commentators was that young people, due to their preoccupation with social media and/ or apathy regarding formal political processes, had failed to enact not only their civic duty but also their global one. Implied here is also that, had young people voted, they could have saved Britain from catastrophe and contributed to maintaining global citizenship through preserving the integrity of existing EU arrangements. This approach positioned young people not only as failing, but also simultaneously as potential *solutions* to problems on a global scale.

Likewise, the Brexit result was also constructed as a warning for young people outside of the United Kingdom, especially young Americans in the lead up to the United States' election and the possibility of a Donald Trump presidency. As one commentator wrote, 'The results of the Brexit referendum shine a light on the importance of the youth vote, and young Americans should learn from them as we approach our own crossroads in November'.[38] Arguably, this public suspicion of young Americans is unfair given that during the election primaries there were many reports that indicated young people were actively rejecting established candidates backing long held party lines, as the *Washington Post* pointed out, 'More young people voted for Bernie Sanders than Trump and Clinton combined—by a lot'.[39] This voting against the two candidates most associated with the two major parties and their existing platforms indicates that young people feel that what matters is not being adequately addressed from the existing political and party systems. At the same time, it shows that their supposed failure to vote could be one way that they are expressing their sense that the existing system is a failure to their generation by actively choosing not to vote for options they see as illegitimate.

Of course, when it comes to discussions of global citizenship young people are not always positioned as failures, and the role of social media in political engagement is not always dismissed. Consequently, in the next section of this chapter we juxtapose this example from the United Kingdom with an example that encourages young people, particularly in the United States, to consume and engage with social media in particular ways in order to be responsible global citizens and win personal material rewards and public recognition.

YOUNG PEOPLE AS GLOBAL CONSUMERS MAKING A DIFFERENCE: BONO'S GLOBAL CITIZEN FESTIVAL

Global Citizen is a platform born out of the Global Poverty Project (GPP), which was launched in 2008 with the aim of ending of extreme poverty. The GPP primarily focuses on developing awareness campaigns to encourage governments, businesses and consumers to take 'simple actions' for change. With the help of substantial publicity through endorsements from high-profile celebrities, such as Bono, the GPP's initiatives claim to have raised millions,[40] helped along by a range of global corporate sponsors such as Cotton On and Coca-Cola.

In 2012, the GPP launched the Global Citizen website, mobile application, and festival. Each year the initiative runs a Global Citizen Festival in Central Park in New York City, to coincide with a UN General Assembly meeting. This is significant as the GPP attempts to align itself with the United Nations as a key authority on global politics. Over the past five years the festival has been host to an array of primarily American and British popular music acts, such as Beyoncé, Jay Z, Coldplay, Ed Sheeran, Foo Fighters, Kendrick Lamar, The Black Keys and Rihanna. Young people are the target of much of the online marketing for the event and the website states that the aim is to 'raise the consciousness of a generation to make change inevitable' through 'an incredible tool to promote activism through something people love—live musical entertainment'.

For a young person to attend the festival, s/he first needs to register to become a 'Global Citizen'. S/he then needs to accrue points by taking actions recognised by the site as in keeping with what a responsible global citizen would do. These actions primarily focus on social media sites, and young people are encouraged to sign petitions, tweet, share information on Facebook about poverty, and send emails to world leaders, among other actions. Once s/he has accrued enough points for these actions, the young person is entered in the draw for festival tickets. This suggests a shift—echoed by the website's images of crowds of young people with their hands in the air in excitement rather than protest—from acts of citizenship based on politics and rights, to acts of citizenship based on online activity and consumption. As young people engage in this way they reflect Koffman, Orgad & Gill's conception of the 'ideal neoliberal subject', one who is 'empowered, agentic, and entrepreneurial'.[41]

During the 2015 Festival, Bono reflected on his own youth and addressed the crowd with a two-minute speech in which he stated that

> 10 years ago, AIDs drugs were just for the rich . . . But I'm proud to tell you, 15 million people you will not likely meet, you are paying for their AIDs drugs. . . . Around here governments have to do what you tell them, if there's enough of you. . . . To own a farm, to own a home, to walk the streets safe from harm, to get connected, to get respected, to pursue their vision and not be suspected, to start a business, to self-esteem, to wake up in your own dream.

This speech suggested that the crowd was directly responsible for paying for the drugs that have helped fifteen million people and constructed that payment as an act of citizenship. In this context, raising awareness is a sort of performance, an act that, through no clear means, enables Global Citizen to raise millions of dollars. But how this money is spent, and how it is possible for this money to absolve systemic issues across state borders, remains unclear. Each fortnight, ticket winners are announced and a new campaign is launched with 'a different challenge for global citizens to solve', creating a narrative in which existing problems are quickly and easily resolved through actions that require minimal resources, time or inconveniences from young people positioned in the Global North.

Ultimately, in his final lines, Bono puts forward the values he sees to be universal: to own property, to walk the streets safely, to start a business, to 'wake up in your own dream'. Such individualised aspirations underpin much of the language used in the platform's promotional material, where being a global citizen is not hard or contentious, but fun and feel-good and ultimately beneficial to you as an individual.

While the Global Citizen platform may be a particularly visible example of the ways actions deemed commercially viable are co-constructed with discourses of global justice, this is not an unusual approach. Indeed, in the next section we take a more detailed look at an Australian example that also positions young global citizens as naturally and inherently in line with the market in the interests of global citizenship, which is constituted as tied to entrepreneurial personal and professional development.

YOUNG PEOPLE AS GLOBAL ENTREPRENEURS WITH ECONOMIC SOLUTIONS: THE FOUNDATION FOR YOUNG AUSTRALIANS

Moving from examples of formal political participation through voting and online activism with material rewards, in this section we examine an example of an organisation that may fall between the two in engaging youth in online platforms as well as programming delivered in physical sites and engagement in policy proposals. Specifically, we look at how young people's global citizenship is conceived by the Foundation for Young Australians (FYA), an organisation that works closely with a network of schools, government, corporations, philanthropists, research institutions and non-governmental organisations. Through an analysis of the ideas and corporate networks that underpin the FYA's website and publication, we find a particular kind of entrepreneurial global citizen is favoured, wherein young people should simultaneously take responsibility for themselves and others, while ensuring Australia's future economic prosperity on a national and global scale.

Formed in 2000 through a partnership between The Queen's Trust (1977–2000) and the Australian Youth Foundation (1987–2000), the FYA was originally a funding body focused on supporting young people from disadvantaged backgrounds. In 2010, with a new CEO, the organisation's focus shifted to an emphasis on becoming what they describe as an 'initiative incubation space focused on education and social change' for all young Australians. Today, FYA is the only national independent non-profit organisation dedicated to young people in Australia. It sits outside traditional educational sites and has come to have significant influence on education in Australia since around the turn of the century. The FYA is supported and funded by a diverse network of schools, government, corporations, philanthropists, research institutions and non-governmental organisations.

While the FYA's work is not solely about global citizenship education, young people are often referred to as global citizens in their material and the FYA's mission on their website states that 'Together, with young people, we want to influence and shape education and career pathways, transform worldviews and lead communities in innovative ways. Together, we want to change the world'. The FYA's website identifies a range of major supporters, and the majority of these are large corporations such as global engineering companies Kentz and Laing O'Rourke, Lotterywest, the National Australia Bank, Samsung, Shell, The Trust Company and The Myer Foundation. The organisation has established its reputation in advocacy, education and research through collaborations with 10,000 educators and 1 million young people and has leveraged over $30 million in investment.[42] As a result, FYA has exercised substantial influence in relation to educational and youth policy in Australia.

Here we focus on the FYA's website and 2013 publication *Unlimited Potential* as representative samples of the discourse most commonly used by the FYA. FYA's website homepage is accessed by diverse audience of potential and current funders, practitioners, young people and other interested members of the public. *Unlimited Potential* includes a number of recommendations and proposals for how key institutions, communities and governments can equip young people for life and work in the twenty-first century. The website and twenty-six-page publication provide information about the work of the organisation and some of their key initiatives, the majority of which centre around young people participating in work experience or volunteering. By examining the contents of both the website and publication, the reader can examine the diverse ways that young people are called upon to be entrepreneurial global citizens and how these intersect and/or compete with the political agendas of the network of institutions that support the FYA's work.

The website strongly reflects an ideology in which business leadership is essential for, and perhaps the most important pathway to, social change. For example, *$20 Boss*, an initiative supported by the National Australia Bank and the Victorian Government, is aimed at inspiring young people to 'be more entrepreneurial whilst creating businesses that make the world a better place'. The initiative is to be run by teachers in schools. Their students are provided with $20 start-up money and are challenged to create their own business. 'It's a fantastic way to engage young people in an immersive experience at school that encourages their entrepreneurial style'.[43] The FYA landing page for this initiative[44] asks, 'What could your students do with $20? The answer might surprise you'. The website also includes a page dedicated to FYA's youth alumni, who hold a range of professional titles, from entrepreneur, director, CEO, to founder, advisor and chair. Such language also reinforces a particular image of the ideal young citizen, whose empowered outlook is closely tied to their position within a corporate trajectory.

According to FYA's CEO, Jan Owen (2013), 'We need young Australians to be confident, connected, enterprising, innovative, optimistic, generous and happy. It begins with an equitable, world class and outward looking education system and the opportunity for young people to engage and become immersed in the real world'. This statement presents a particular image of what young Australians ought to aspire to be or become. Throughout the publication, in contrast to deficit models often applied to young people (as in when they were blamed for Brexit outcomes, for example), the FYA uses a different array of attributes to describe young people, who they see as: agile, enterprising, engaging, inspiring, empowered, persistent, resilient, willing, imaginative, optimistic, happy, confident, creative, passionate, effective, aware, active, generous, innovative, courageous and resourceful. Youth are spoken of as a 'source of energy', a 'driving force', as 'comfortable with change' and 'technology savvy' and with 'untapped talent'. This language frames young people in relation to their ability to both solve global problems and enhance business relationships and works to produce a particular kind of subject constituted in accordance with their commercial value. In other words, the vision presented here privileges attributes that are appealing to the needs of business and technology.

The website also highlights case studies of individual young people who have participated in FYA initiatives. Aside from an occasional photograph of a small group of young people in the same room or studio, the website and publication focus on stories of individual young people rather than examples of collective action. Suggesting young people have individual responsibility over their own lives while also requiring that they be responsible for particular corporate or political needs points to a fundamental tension within such approaches to youth and global citizenship. In this context, for example, youth are expected to 'create the world they want to live in' while also 'meeting the demands of Australia's future economy'.[45] Likewise, youth citizenship is instrumentalised for the economic growth it may produce: 'The predicted benefits [of youth engaging with Asia] are startling. For example, it is predicted that Australia could potentially lift its economic performance by up to $275 billion over the next 10 years through closer ties with Asia'.

Such language moves the focus from the young person's needs to the needs of the economy or at least relies on the belief that the two are intimately connected and co-constructed. The website provides specific examples of youth developing projects such as 'enterprise with a social purpose' and participating in activities such as work placements in which they meet stockbrokers. Such examples place the emphasis on entrepreneurial aspirations coupled with their ability to govern themselves. While there is at least one example focusing not on market goals and responsibilities but rather on learning about and connecting with other cultures, making friends and being motivated for university, in this case too the focus remains on individual rather than collective gains. In constructing young people as individual entrepreneurs ready to solve problems through participation in the global market, the document presents a neoliberal view of a young person's national and global responsibilities built on market demands.

CRITICALLY ANALYSING NEOLIBERAL CONCEPTIONS OF GLOBAL CITIZENSHIP

Neoliberal discourses of young people can perpetuate inequality by expecting young people from the Global North to save the world, while simultaneously projecting 'their beliefs and myths as universal and reproduc[ing] power relations and violence similar to those in colonial times'.[46] Given this framing, Andreotti advocates for an approach to global citizenship that encourages young people to engage in a more critical, active way that recognises notions of power, inequality and difference.

Through looking critically at these various approaches to youth global citizenship, we suggest that the dominant discourse of neoliberalism has created a variety of other subjugated knowledges in the process of producing particular kinds of entrepreneurial global citizens. By 'subjugated knowledges' we refer to the ideas that become subordinated or marginalised when other viewpoints come to dominate. Consequently, it is worth asking how subjugated knowledges occur when the neoliberal, entrepreneurial vision of the responsible global citizen is emphasised in relation to youth and how this plays out in global citizenship education.

One area of subjugated knowledge includes those global responsibilities that sit outside of, or even compete with, neoliberal political or corporate agendas. As already indicated in the above analyses, common discourses of global citizenship assume that what young people desire or ought to desire is what will also be what is 'best' for the nation—in rational economic terms and vice versa. There is a notion that the world in which young people want to live and work will be in agreement with perpetual economic growth and individual advancement. This subjugates different knowledge of young people who may not be able, or desire, to fit into this entrepreneurial persona.

The dominant neoliberal rendering of young people's global citizenship also potentially subjugates research and perspectives that take a more critical stance on global citizenship. For example, research that suggests a global vision should work towards the opposite of economic growth, that is, a 'degrowth economy'[47] that involves producing and consuming *less* not more in order to respond to the environmental issues of our times would struggle to find space for incorporation in this discourse.[48] So too would be an approach to global citizenship that fosters critical discourse and challenges rather than supports and promotes colonial systems of power.[49]

A focus that disproportionately prioritises individual responsibilities of young people also has the potential to depoliticise the notion of global citizenship, which in turn may override or indeed reproduce systemic forms of inequality that exist within and between nation-states. Through the privileging of corporate objectives in needing to attend to donor interests, global citizenship initiatives may often obscure a significant body of actions and scholarship that maintain the need for a critical perspective on the neoliberal discourses that position young people as entrepreneurial citizens.

LOOKING TO THE FUTURE: CONSTRAINTS AND POSSIBILITIES

The young person as a global citizen has developed into a popular vision in the twenty-first century, one supported and disseminated by an increasingly diverse network of actors beyond the nation-state. This chapter has focused on how this global vision is expressed across recent examples in the United Kingdom, the United States, Oxford, and Australia. In taking this focus, this chapter aims not to cast judgment on whether these examples are 'good' or 'bad', but rather to consider the effects of the underlying discourses by which young people are constituted. Following Foucault, we agree that '[a] critique does not consist in saying that things aren't good the way they are. It consists in seeing on just what type of assumptions, of familiar notions, of established and unexamined ways of thinking the accepted practices are based'.[50]

Overall the three examples examined in this chapter demonstrate how young people and their global responsibilities are constructed through a neoliberal lens, whereby engagement with the world based on individual actions, entrepreneurship and job market participation are privileged, while approaches that are more collective and concerned with challenging systemic issues are downplayed or ignored.

When asking such questions we also recognise the practical constraints and material realities youth organisations and movements face. It is understandable that options are constrained in an environment in which organisations must compete for funding from bodies that may not place value on the sort of critical reflection that potentially works against an entrepreneurial model. Moving forward in research and practice will thus require critical reflection while also taking into account the realities of global networks. From this starting point we aim to move towards offering new approaches that challenge but also engage with existing assumptions in order to better recognise and support young people's diverse interests, needs and efforts as global citizens and to explore how these approaches might translate into a more rounded citizenship education for young people both inside and outside of schools.

NOTES

1. Lettevall, R. and Klockar Linder, M. (Eds.) (2008). 'The idea of kosmopolis: history, philosophy and politics of world citizenship'. *Södertörn Academic Studies* **37**, Södertörns högskola.

2. Brysk, A. (2002). 'Conclusion: from rights to realities'. In A. Brysk (Ed.), *Globalisation and Human Rights* (pp. 242–256). California: University of California Press. @ 243.

3. UNESCO. (2014). Global citizenship education. Retrieved August 15, 2016, from www.unesco.org/new/en/global-citizenship-education.

4. Gaudelli, W. and W. R. Fernekes. (2004). 'Teaching about global human rights for global citizenship'. *The Social Studies* **95** (1): 16–26.

5. Lansdown, G. (2010). The realisation of children's participation rights:critical reflections'. In B. P. Smith and N. Thomas (eds.) *A Handbook of Children and Young People's Participation.* London: Routledge. @ 11–23.

6. Freeman, M. (1998). 'The sociology of childhood and children's rights'. *The International Journal of Children's Rights* **6** (4): 433–444.

7. Stasiulis, D. (2002). 'The active child citizen: lessons from Canadian policy and the children's movement'. *Citizenship Studies* **6** (4): 507–538. @ 2.

8. See, for example:Suárez-Orozco, M. M. and C. Sattin. (2007). 'Wanted: global citizens'. *Educational Leadership* **64** (7): 58–62; Bourn, D. (2010). 'Students as Global Citizens'. In E. Jones (Ed.) *Internationalisation and the Student Voice: Higher Education Perspectives.* London: Routledge. @ 18–29; Braskamp, L. A. (2008). 'Developing global citizens'. *Journal of College and Character* **10** (1): 1–5; Nussbaum, M. (2004). 'Liberal education and global community'. *Liberal Education* **90** (1): 42–47.

9. See, for example:Veugelers, W. (2011). 'The moral and the political in global citizenship: appreciating differences in education'. *Globalisation, Societies and Education* **9** (3–4): 473–485.Gerzon, M. (2010). *American Citizen, Global Citizen.* Boulder, CO, SpiritScope Publishing.Schattle, H. (2008). 'Education for global citizenship: illustrations of ideological pluralism and adaptation'. *Journal of Political Ideologies* **13** (1): 73–94.

10. Parker, W. C., Ninomiya, A. & Cogan, J. J. (2002). 'Educating"world citizens": toward multinational curriculum development. In W. C. Parker (Ed.), *Education for Democracy: Contexts, Curricula, Assessments* (pp. 151–184). Greenwich, CT, Information Age Publishing.

11. Ruddick, S. (2003). 'The politics of aging: globalization and the restructuring of youth and childhood'. *Antipode*, **35** (2): 334–362. @ 357.

12. Ibid.

13. See, for example: Tsaliki, C., Frangonikolopoulos, C. & Huliaras, A. (2011). *Transnational Celebrity Activism in Global politics: Changing the World?* Chicago: University of Chicago Press; UNESCO. (2014). Global citizenship education. Retrieved August 15, 2016, from www.unesco.org/new/en/global-citizenship-education; Kelly, P. & Harrison, L. (2009). *Working in Jamie's Kitchen: Salvation, Passion and Young Workers.* Hampshire: Palgrave Macmillan.

14. Pruitt, L. J. (2013). ' "Fixing the Girls": neoliberal discourse and girls' participation in peacebuilding'. *International Feminist Journal of Politics* **15** (1): 58–76.

15. Couldry, N. (2010). *Why Voice Matters: Culture and Politics After Neoliberalism.* London: Sage Publications Ltd.

16. See Pruitt, L. J. (2013).

17. Fisher, T. (2006). 'Race, neoliberalism, and "Welfare Reform" in Britain'. *Social Justice* **33** (3): 54–65.

18. Lakes, R. D. and P. A. Carter (2011). 'Neoliberalism and education: an introduction'. *Educational Studies* **47** (2): 107–110.

19. Koffman, O., S. Orgad and R. Gill (2015). 'Girl power and "selfie humanitarianism"'. *Continuum: Journal of Media & Cultural Studies* **29** (2): 157–168. @ 161.

20. Koffman, O. and R. Gill (2013). ' "The revolution will be led by a 12-year-old girl": girl power and global biopolitics'. *Feminist Review* **103**: 83–102. @ 92.

21. Ibid. @ 94.

22. Berents, H. (2016). 'Hashtagging girlhood: #IAmMalala, #BringBackOurGirls and gendering representations of global politics'. *International Feminist Journal of Politics*. @ 12.

23. Arnot, M. (2009). *Educating the Gendered Citizen: Sociological Engagements with National and Global Agendas*. London, Routledge. @ 227.

24. Peters, M. (2001). 'Education, enterprise culture and the entrepreneurial self: a Foucauldian perspective'. *Journal of Educational Enquiry* 2(2): 58–71.

25. Rose, N. (1996). 'The death of the social: reconfiguring the territory of government'. *Economy & Society* **25**, 327–366. @ 44.

26. Lemke, J. L. (2001) 'Articulating communities: sociocultural perspectives on science education'. *Journal of Research in Science Teaching* **38**: 296–316. @ 201.

27. Kelly, P. & Harrison, L. (2009). *Working in Jamie's Kitchen: Salvation, Passion and Young Workers*. Hampshire: Palgrave Macmillan. @ 9.

28. http://www.bbc.com/news/politics/eu_referendum/results

29. *The Independent* (2016, 30 June) 'Theresa May's Tory leadership launch statement: full text'. Accessed 10 July 2016 from http://www.independent.co.uk/news/uk/politics/theresa-mays-tory-leadership-launch-statement-full-text-a7111026.html.

30. Fung, B. (2016, June 24). 'The British are frantically Googling what the E.U. is, hours after voting to leave it'. *The Washington Post*. Accessed 15 July: https://www.washingtonpost.com/news/the-switch/wp/2016/06/24/the-british-are-frantically-googling-what-the-eu-is-hours-after-voting-to-leave-it/.

31. Versi, M. (2016, 27 June) 'Brexit has given voice to racism—and too many are complicit'. *The Guardian*. Accessed 15 July 2016 from https://www.theguardian.com/commentisfree/2016/jun/27/brexit-racism-eu-referendum-racist-incidents-politicians-media.

32. Cited in Parkinson, H. J. (2016, 28 June) 'Young people are so bad at voting—I'm disappointed in my peers'. *The Guardian*. Accessed 15 July 2016 from https://www.theguardian.com/commentisfree/2016/jun/28/young-people-bad-voting-millennials-eu-vote-politics.

33. Helm, T. (2016, 10 July) 'EU Referendum: youth turnout almost twice as high as first thought'. *The Guardian*. Accessed 15 July 2016 from http://www.theguardian.com/politics/2016/jul/09/young-people-referendum-turnout-brexit-twice-as-high?CMP=Share_iOSApp_Other

34. Cited in Cresci, E. and Guardian readers (2016, 24 June) 'Meet the 75%: the young people who voted to remain in the EU'. *The Guardian*. Accessed 15 July 2016 from http://www.theguardian.com/politics/2016/jun/24/meet-the-75-young-people-who-voted-to-remain-in-eu

35. ABC News (2015, 25 June). 'Brexit: Young Britons use social media to declare the EU referendum result #NotInMyName'. Accessed 10 July 2016 from http://www.abc.net.au/news/2016-06-25/young-brits-declare-brexit-result-not-in-my-name/7543316.

36. Parkinson, H. J. (2016, 28 June) 'Young people are so bad at voting—I'm disappointed in my peers'. *The Guardian*. Accessed 15 July 2016 from https://www.theguardian.com/commentisfree/2016/jun/28/young-people-bad-voting-millennials-eu-vote-politics

37. Prendergast, L. (2016, 25 June). 'Brexit was a harsh political awakening for young people'. *The Spectator*. Accessed 28 June from http://blogs.spectator.co.uk/2016/06/brexit-political-awakening-young-people/

38. Rodriguez, G. (2016, 24 June) 'Brexit is a warning to young American voters'. *The National Memo*. Accessed 13 July 2016 from http://www.nationalmemo.com/brexit-is-a-warning-to-young-american-voters/

39. Blake, A. (2016, 20 June) 'More young people voted for Bernie Sanders than Trump and Clinton combined—by a lot' *Washington Post*. Accessed 28 June from https://www.washingtonpost.com/news/the-fix/wp/2016/06/20/more-young-people-voted-for-bernie-sanders-than-trump-and-clinton-combined-by-a-lot/

40. Global Citizen (2016) Global Citizen: Impact [website]. Accessed 28 June from: https://www.globalcitizen.org/en/impact/

41. Koffman, O., S. Orgad and R. Gill (2015). 'Girl power and "selfie humanitarianism"'. *Continuum: Journal of Media & Cultural Studies* **29** (2): 157–168. @ 165.

42. Foundation for Young Australians (2014). Foundation for Young Australians website. www.fya.org.au. Accessed: 15/10/2014.

43. Quote from the FYA $20 Boss webpage. http://www.fya.org.au/our-programs/20boss/. Last accessed October 3, 2016.

44. Ibid.

45. Foundation for Young Australians (2013) *Unlimited Potential: A Commitment to Young Australians*. Melbourne: FYA.

46. Andreotti, V. (2006). 'Soft versus critical global citizenship education'. *Policy and Practice—A Development Education Review* **3**: 40–51. @ 41.

47. Schneider, F., G. Kallis, and J. Martinez-Alier. (2010). 'Crisis or opportunity? Economic degrowth for social equity and ecological sustainability'. *Journal of Cleaner Production* **18** (6): 511–518.

48. Alexander, S. (2014). 'Life in a "degrowth" economy, and why you might actually enjoy it'. *The Conversation*. Accessed 13 July from https://theconversation.com/life-in-a-degrowth-economy-and-why-you-might-actually-enjoy-it-32224

49. Andreotti, V. (2006). 'Soft versus critical global citizenship education'. *Policy and Practice—A Development Education Review* **3**: 40–51.

50. Foucault, M. (1981). So is it important to think? In J. D. Faubion (Ed.) *Power: Essential Works of Foucault* 1954–1984 (R. Hurley, trans, pp. 454–458). New York: New Press. @ 456.

Chapter Six

Co-designed

A New Approach to Civics and Citizenship

Mark Chou and Jean-Paul Gagnon

So often, as we have now shown in this book, the issue of youth political disengagement is one that is analysed primarily through a deficit discourse. Policymakers and curriculum experts tend to focus on what young people are not doing and what they appear not to know as the basis of their political engagement with youth. What results is as familiar as it is worrying. Portrayed as the problem or cause of a country's civic deficit, young people often find themselves the subjects of policy initiatives and educational programmes designed by experts to instil in them the right attitudes and aspirations that may one day allow them to become full citizens—even global citizens. This is how a civic deficit is transformed into a potential civic surplus: by ensuring young people are treated as 'citizens in the making' and restricted to a 'developmental path' devised to inspire them to see the benefits of participating in legitimate, formal practices of politics, from voting at elections, contacting politicians to joining political parties.[1]

But such an approach, even when successful, remains problematic to the extent that it delegitimises certain young people and their political activities as deficient and delinquent until or unless they have managed the transition from citizens in the making to full citizens. Seeing youth political disengagement from a civic deficit perspective thus underscores the view that young people are responsible for causing an impending future crisis of democracy, a crisis which can only be averted with appropriate expert policy and curriculum intervention. Privileging formal political practices also diminishes the so-called new politics of young people which, according to youth researchers Judith Bessant, Rys Farthing and Rob Watts, tends to be more interactive, creative, everyday and non-hierarchical.[2] It is a politics that, as we have reiterated, can seem apolitical or even anti-political when viewed from the perspective of mainstream understandings of what political participation is.

Needless to say, this is a politics which most policy and curriculum experts have also overlooked and often dismissed.

In this chapter we make the case that this is a mistake. Following scholars like Therese O'Toole, David Marsh and Su Jones, we believe that a new approach is needed to evaluate the relationship between youth civic deficit, the crisis of democracy and civics education. As they put it, when 'concern about youth political disengagement is focused on an impending future crisis of political participation and on the failure to induct young people effectively into "adult politics", rather than on the failure to engage with young people and with the issues that affect and concern them', we not only undermine youth politically, branding them as deficient, but also throw away a potentially fruitful opportunity to learn from them and to work in partnership with them.[3] As we see it, the problem is not with policy and curriculum experts wanting to turn a civic deficit into a civic surplus. Nor is it necessarily with educators hoping that civics education may act as a vehicle for this transformation to occur. The problem is with how deficit and surplus have conventionally been defined and understood. If what has traditionally been labelled as a deficit may in fact be in-and-of-itself considered a surplus, then it may be the case that some young people already possess what they—and others—require to creatively redefine the 'substance, forms, and limits of democracy'.[4]

The point is this: yes, there are some young people who because of their political activism or lack thereof have been deemed responsible for causing a crisis of democracy (as defined by mainstream, formal political participation). At the same time, though, there also are many young people who have been challenging, reinvigorating and re-defining democracy and its so-called crisis through their own politics. In doing so, they have shown that democratic crises can actually offer an important stimulus for democratic renewal.

What lessons can policy and curriculum experts learn from this when it comes to designing and implementing civics education? While curriculum matters are often the most resistant of any facet of education to change and reform,[5] civics curriculum included, we put forward a proposal in this chapter based around the notion of co-design. This is an approach to curriculum that argues that young people should ideally be incorporated as 'co-investigators' and 'co-producers' in the entire civics curricula design and implementation process so that they can see themselves as 'equal stakeholders' of an education and civics platform that better resonates with their own political inclinations, not just those of mainstream policy and curriculum authorities. To turn a deficit into a surplus—or rather to see a deficit as a potential surplus—it is incumbent on authorities and experts to build young people into the discussions and decision-making. When this is done, civics education will both be better equipped to recognise and potentially redress 'the raft of barriers to young people's political participation'.[6] Indeed, who better to ask about youth political dis/engagement than young people themselves? What better way to ensure a curriculum is framed to facilitate young people's citizenship and participation in politics, both in terms of mainstream understandings *and* in newly emerging contexts, than to have youth involved in the design and implementation process?

This chapter proceeds in three sections. First, we will begin our discussion with a brief overview of what conventionally happens when it comes to civics curricula design and implementation. This process which we will demonstrate is one driven almost exclusively by experts with little effort to consult with young people, let alone building them into each stage of the expert process—from its origins in public administration through to current efforts to incorporate it into civics curricula design. Finally, we end this chapter with a broader reflection on what it takes to ensure that a school and its civics curriculum becomes democratic and whether these structural shifts can positively influence students in terms of their citizenship and political practices in the decades to come.

AN EXPERT'S CONFESSION: CONVENTIONAL APPROACHES TO CURRICULUM DESIGN AND IMPLEMENTATION

In most Anglo-American countries, the school is considered the primary institution responsible for the education, development and well-being of society's young people. Given the significance of this social institution, decisions about what to teach, and how to teach it, are always fiercely contested—by government officials, policymakers, teachers, pedagogical and curriculum bodies, academics and parents as well. But despite having become more consultative in recent decades, important pedagogical and curriculum decisions have remained the preserve of education experts and policymakers. This has been no truer than of how civics curricula have been designed and implemented in countries such as the United Kingdom, the United States and Australia. As Bessant, Farthing and Watts note, '[t]here is a long tradition of thought that if we want to revitalise and sustain democratic citizenship, increasing levels of civic knowledge and information is something best done by experts working in the education system'.[7]

Against the widespread concerns heard over the past several decades regarding the declining interest and capacity of young people in these countries to engage with politics, schools have frequently been singled out as the key social institution that has been failing to cultivate in young people the basic civic skills they need, as citizens, to thrive in a democracy.[8] While the family unit and other community organisations have also been discussed in this context,[9] governments have invested most of their time and funding into school-based initiatives designed to redress this apparent civic deficit. The key reason for this is that research has shown that civic knowledge and political engagement are things best promoted within the school setting.[10] Faced with mounting social and political pressures to stem the 'high levels of citizen disaffection with politics', 'gross lack of political literacy' and 'low levels of satisfaction and trust in [government]',[11] which many contemporary policy analysts see as a 'reflection of a deepening crisis of democracy',[12] governments have thus called for an urgent revival of civics education as part of the school curriculum. In the United Kingdom, the United States and Australia, wave after wave of civics renewal, costing hundreds of millions of government funding, has been proposed and implemented.[13]

In almost all cases, the approach favoured by governments when it comes to designing curriculum has been one where educational experts are either consulted by government or called in to analyse the issue and to decide on behalf of young people what they need to learn and how they should learn it. There is an assumption that only those who possess the appropriate level of professional expertise and experience should be tasked with the job of determining what type of education young people need. These are the people who are in the position to represent what young people require and as such dictate to them what and how they need to learn. Young people, who have acquired neither the requisite knowledge nor life experience, must be excluded from such debates.

There are many case studies we can refer to here to illustrate this approach to civics curricula design, but perhaps one of the most prominent examples is the Civics Expert Group (CEG) that was convened by the Australian government in 1994 to review the state of civics education in the country. Specifically, at the request of then Prime Minister Paul Keating, the CEG was requested 'to prepare a strategic plan for a non-partisan program of public education on civic issues' for the purposes of ensuring 'that Australians can participate fully in civic decision-making processes'.[14] What the CEG found, as was documented in their report *Whereas the People . . . Civics and Citizenship Education*, is that 'effective' citizenship requires 'an informed citizenry; without active, knowledgeable citizens the forms of democratic representation remain empty; without vigilant, informed citizens there is no check on potential tyranny'.[15] To ensure this happens, they proposed that any model of the good citizen be premised on their

> knowledge and understanding of Australia's political and social heritage, its democratic processes and government, its judicial system and its system of public administration. In the absence of an adequate understanding of how our society works, without the skills and confidence to participate effectively and the encouragement to do so, they simply cannot be effective citizens.[16]

In reaching this decision, the CEG—a body comprised of some of Australia's foremost social and political experts—consulted widely. They invited and received close to two hundred submissions from interested individuals and bodies, as well as others with vested interests in Australian politics and education. But despite their efforts at inclusion, at no point did the CEG consult with or include young people themselves.

As Stuart Macintyre, who chaired the CEG, later conceded in an essay titled 'An Expert's Confession', the Group consulted all affected parties except the young people who would ultimately be most impacted by their recommendations. The consultation process, which Macintyre describes in detail, is worth replicating here given the point we are emphasising. As he puts it:

> In response to the advertisements, we received 180 submissions. Many of those who made them wished to meet with us and in addition we needed to meet with others. We made trips to each of the states and territories, and talked to ministers, directors of education and their staff, officers of teachers' unions and parents' organisations, the Curriculum Council of Educational Research, teachers and teacher educators, governors, party leaders, the Australian Local Government Association, the Australian Electoral Commission and Parliamentary Education Office, the Western Australian Constitutional Committee, the Centenary of Federation Advisory Committee, the Aboriginal and Torres Strait Islander Commission, Federation of Ethnic Communities' Councils, Office of Multicultural Affairs, the Constitutional Centenary Foundation, Project: Citizenship 2001 and the Australasian Political Studies Association.[17]

What this extensive list demonstrates is something important: the CEG took its job very seriously. The only thing which it perhaps did not take seriously enough was the views of young people themselves. Now more than two decades old, the legacy left by this landmark report continues to shape debates about civics education in Australia. Indeed, recent Australian Curriculum, Assessment and Reporting Authority (ACARA) approaches to civics design continue to emphasise the importance of formal understandings of politics. Not only that, they continue to rely largely on the advice of 'curriculum experts, stage of schooling specialists and others with extensive research and practical experience in this domain', including 'parents, teachers, professional associations, community groups, academics and state territory authorities'—everyone beside young people it would seem.[18]

In short, this exemplifies the conventional approach to civics curricula design and implementation in many countries. Experts take charge while young people are marginalised if not excluded. Whereas the former are agents in the process, the latter are merely treated as the subjects. In this way, the appropriate role of young people as students is merely one of 'compliance and acceptance: adherence to what is prescribed, asked, or offered by the adults in charge'.[19] Because experts assume young people are uninterested in or incapable of offering insights into civic competency and education, they have rejected more participatory and inclusive approaches to curriculum design for reifying the views of the uninformed and inexperienced.[20] This, as we now demonstrate, amounts to an important opportunity missed to engage as well as educate young people about civics and citizenship.

THE PRACTICE OF CO-DESIGN

According to many scholars in education, youth studies and political participation, it is hardly surprising to find that many young people feel they are poorly represented when it comes to important decisions and policies, even ones that directly affect their lives.[21] Whether at the local or national level, young people frequently convey a sense of exclusion from community debates. The simple reason for this is because they are. As O'Toole, Marsh and Jones' research shows, 'young people are rarely consulted or listened to—even with respect to issues which directly affect them, such as the introduction of AS levels, the types of training course they could access on the New Deal, decisions about local amenities or community events and so on'.[22] This exclusion not only exacerbates the problem of youth political disengagement, it has also been proven to be a bad policy and decision-making practice.[23]

As part of the so-called citizen-centred revolution in public administration and service delivery, the practice of 'co-design' (and also 'co-production') has become increasingly popular among government agencies seeking to improve service provider–client relationships.[24] What underpins this shift in policy practice is the notion that those who are most affected by a decision or policy should have the greatest say during the design, production and implementation phases.[25] Indeed, 'children and young people's participation' in public policy 'has never before been a more popular policy demand'.[26] By giving stakeholders a greater say in what takes place, it helps to ensure that 'government policies, programmes and services be organized around the needs and priorities of the people, businesses and organizations they serve, rather than those of governments'.[27] But what makes co-design distinctive is that it is neither top-down nor bottom-up. Co-design is interactive: it is based on a mutually dependent partnership between government and citizens who must show each other trust, respect, openness and responsibility.[28] Specifically, the practice of co-design is premised on three key elements.[29] First, citizens must want to be involved in decisions about important public policies and government must provide meaningful opportunities and arrangements for such citizen participation to occur. Either one on its own will mean that co-design will not reach its fullest potential. Second, for co-design to work, citizens must be prepared to do more than air their own personal grievances. They must be willing to come informed and to discuss ideas openly. Co-design is in its essence an exchange of ideas. Third, while co-design can be ad hoc, the best practices tend to have available to them a permanent institutional arrangement that is publicly known for fostering citizen participation.

There are several potential political implications of co-design. The first is that it ensures the relationship between government and citizens becomes more horizontal rather than hierarchical.[30] Of course, the ultimate power often still rests with government. They still control the funds and how policies are implemented and reformed. Yet co-design is an important safeguard to ensure the needs of citizens are met and their wishes are actually represented by their supposed political representatives. In this regard, co-design is an essential practice in representative democracies.[31] A second political implication flowing from co-design is that, through the dialogue and collective deliberation that must take place, governments not only become better attuned to the desires of citizens, citizens also get a better understanding of some of the pressures and limitations faced by those in government. This is important because many citizens in Western democracies often assume politicians are lazy, corrupt and incapable of fulfilling the promises they made at election time. While there is some truth in these claims, few citizens appreciate how difficult governing can be. Democratic politics is a messy and time-consuming affair. It is a game of give-and-take, of compromises. Incorporating more citizens into this process through the practice of co-design can thus help to demystify the policymaking process and in turn ensure that more realistic understandings and expectations of politicians emerge as a result. The third implication of co-design is that citizens who are involved in the design, production and implementation of policy will be more likely to have a vested interest in complying with that policy when it is implemented.[32] In other words, citizens will take greater responsibility for their own well-being and the health of their community. They will be more engaged when it comes to ensuring what they have worked on works not just for themselves, but for others as well.

Why this is such a drastic break from traditional service delivery and policymaking is because co-design does not to treat citizens as passive recipients or mere subjects. Traditional policy practices, which were largely top-down affairs, saw the service provider–client/government–citizen relationship as one of 'superior–subordinate'.[33] Indeed, as Frank Fischer notes, the relationship was a very specific and non-responsive one. 'On the professional side of this understanding', writes Fischer, 'experts agree to deliver their services to the limits of their competence, to respect the confidences of their clients, and not to misuse for their own benefit the special powers accorded to them by the relationship'.[34] As for the client or citizen in this equation, they 'agree to accept the professional's authority in specific areas of expertise, to submit to the professional's ministrations, and, of course, to pay for services rendered'. Clients and citizens were not to be consulted or treated as equals because they lacked the expertise and experience of policy professionals or the professional politician. Because of this, the interaction was simply one-way: from the expert to the masses. Co-design, guided by its citizen-centred principles, turns this on its head.

Networked and distributed, egalitarian and creative, co-design envisages that there is no better expertise than that which is grounded in ordinary social experience. To ensure people remain engaged and vested in government, government must actively ask 'what people want and are capable of, rather than at the top with what systems and policies want and have available to spend'.[35] This is how citizens on the street can become policymakers, bureaucrats and researchers in their own right.

But whereas the practice of co-design has seen widespread application in various public sectors and services, the key problem is that to date it remains underutilised with respect to young people and youth-related services. Where it has been applied to youth matters, such as civics education, it continues to involve only adults as partners—something which the CEG and ARACA examples depict well. This needs to change, we argue, because young people are uniquely placed to offer up the best knowledge and understandings of issues affecting their daily lives.

But for co-design to work for young people, governments must do more than 'getting young people involved in prosocial ways in education, training and community life'.[36] According to researchers such as Philippa Collin, Ariadne Vromen and Girish Lala, for example, existing approaches to incorporating young people into policymaking tends to privilege conventional, adult-driven practices. When they are not tokenistic, to borrow the words of Anita Harris and Joanna Wyn, they do little to overcome existing power relations that marginalise young people.[37] Because of this, there needs to be a commitment to re-envisioning engagement in terms of 'listening to, understanding and collaborating with young people in policy processes'.[38] Co-designing with young people requires nothing less than a concerted effort by the government's public service providers to create 'strategies for communication and decision-making that are responsive to young people's expectations and capacities'.

Indeed, what the latest research tells us is that young people are often politically disengaged or apathetic only because decision-makers continue to treat them as such. The persistent view of young people as lacking the knowledge and capacity to inform policy is less a diagnosis than a continued cause for their political alienation. To combat these tendencies, policy experts and politicians should rethink how they see young people and approach decisions made about them. For researchers at Australia's Young and Well cooperative Research Centre, due to these considerations, it is important for adults to consider at least six basic guiding principles when seeking to collaborate with young people.[39] First, engagement with young people should be premised on an evidence-based approach but one that is flexible enough to change to the specific circumstances and participants. Second, engagement should ideally be collaborative or youth-led where possible, instead of always being adult-led or consultative. Importantly, young people should have space to engage each other without feeling watched by adults. Third, engagement based on 'multiple and diverse' methods is highly preferred to conventional consultative boards or representatives. Given that young people's politics is often networked and creative, a truly collaborative exercise needs to talk this talk and walk this walk. Fourth, technology-based engagement is considered highly effective among young people. Such forms of engagement better reflect young people's daily lived experiences and plays to their expertise. Fifth, engagement must be culturally attuned. Like engaging adults, different approaches are sometimes needed when working with individuals and groups from different cultural or ethnic backgrounds. The same applies to young people. Finally, youth engagement must be adequately resourced from all involved stakeholders, from government and business through to youth-related organisations. This is to ensure all stakeholders have a vested interest in the process and outcomes.

Underpinning these guiding principles is the realisation that young people are actually already full citizens, not citizens in the making. They can make their own decisions and offer important insights especially into policies affecting areas of society in which they spend the most time. However, as Bessant cautions, just because young people are full citizens does not mean they are the same as their more elderly and experienced equivalents. 'While arguing a case for enhanced recognition of young peoples' actual competencies', she concedes that 'it also needs to be acknowledged that by virtue of their age and relative inexperience, young people are frequently more vulnerable than experienced adults, and for this reason require some protection or guardianship'[40]—much like the Preamble to the *United Nations Convention on the Rights of the Child* beseeches parents and guardians to do. Young people, many of whom are already engaged in their own public spheres, may therefore need extra encouragement and care when entering adult-sponsored institutions. But when these measures are in place, there is nothing to suggest that young people cannot make an invaluable, engaged and considered political contribution.

CO-DESIGNING CIVICS CURRICULA: YOUNG PEOPLE,
CIVICS EDUCATION AND POLITICAL ENGAGEMENT

Already in policy areas such as mental health, homelessness, urban planning and economic development, we have seen the type of contributions young people are capable of making when provided with adequate encouragement and care by government officials.[41] These innovative policy practices are something we believe could be extended to the realm of education, in particular to the design and implementation of civics curricula. If the practice of co-design is applied to civics education, it would help to inform policymakers and curriculum experts of the new politics of young people, not just the conventional forms of politics which they are more accustomed to.[42] With more first-hand interactions with the subjects of their analysis—many of whom would transition from passive subjects to more active agents in the process—policymakers and curriculum experts unlock the potential to co-produce with young people a curriculum that is more in tune with the lived realities of today's young people rather than merely replicating unhelpful stereotypes.

Obviously, not all co-designed experiments will lead to workable results. That is the nature of collaborative policy projects—they can be messy and will not always end with useable products. Moreover, the relative inexperience of young people and their lack of curriculum expertise remains a potential limitation with respect to how readily their insights can be translated into actual curriculum policy. Yet scholars have noted that particularly when it comes to co-design, inexperience may actually be a good thing. According to the governance scholar Gerry Stoker for instance, while the policy inexperience of young people is usually considered by experts a cause for concern, there are potential advantages. As he notes, inexperience with the policy process can be a benefit because young people tend to be 'more open to the prospects for change and doing things differently'.[43] Before youth have been socialised into acquiring acceptable forms of behaviours and proposing the right type of policies by government institutions and policy processes, their views are much more fluid and proposals more creative than many of their more senior and experienced equivalents. Rather than a problem to be solved, inexperience can produce true innovation. At least for scholars like Stoker, then, it is not the experienced but rather inexperienced who are less likely to feel disenchantment with politics and the political system. These are the people we need informing the policies about our school's civics curricula.

There is a wide variety of different ways young people have already engaged with the curriculum policymaking process. In particular, young people have participated extensively as student researchers and inquirers, as producers and co-producers and as co-authors and co-creators in teaching and learning.[44] Though many of these experiments have taken place in the context of higher rather than primary K–12 education settings,[45] they offer fruitful examples of why it is important to incorporate the views of young people into the curricula which will ultimately impact how and what they learn.

On the whole though, young people have tended only to be involved in one of two broad categories of curricula design.[46] The first category is where they engage in learning, teaching and research through inquiries into subject content and assessment. The second category is where they engage in learning and teaching policies through inquiries into curriculum design and pedagogic design. There are numerous examples of young people being involved in the first category of teaching engagement but unfortunately far fewer instances where young people have had opportunities to participate in the second category. As Mick Healey, Abbi Flint and Kathy Harrington note of practices in Britain, the consensus seems to be that young people 'are commonly engaged in course evaluations and in departmental staff–student communications, but it is rarer for institutions to go beyond the student voice and engage students as partners in designing the curriculum and giving pedagogic advice and consultancy'.[47] While they argue that this imbalance is already improving, it still remains the case that the majority of young people continued to be marginalised in the curriculum design process.

To change this, we argue that policymakers and curriculum designers need a better framework for working with young people. While there are many protocols they can follow, here we offer a way forward that will help authorities collaborate with young people and enable them to engage at different levels in different ways.

To begin with, a co-designed civics curriculum should at a minimum be premised on asking and answering two key questions. The first is *how do young people evaluate the civics education they currently receive in their schools?* While extensive research has considered what senior educators and experts think constitutes an effective civics education, researchers must directly ask this question of a diverse group of young people. Indeed, young people's visibility and voice must not only appear after the fact—through national proficiency tests used to assess the effectiveness of a particular civics curriculum. Their perspectives must be present at all stages of the debate and development of effective and relevant school-based civics programmes. This makes even more sense as young people are often the innovators in newer forms of political engagement. The second question to ask is *how might civics education better account for young people's understandings and practices of citizenship and political participation?* While many existing civics curricula tend to emphasise that a civics education should be the sum of 'class-based activities, whole-school activities and community activities'[48] young people's input is needed to determine how this can and should occur. Policymakers and curriculum experts can draw on the insights gleaned from the first question to then engage with young people to explore how 'student citizenship in a school and community context' that contributes to the strengthening democracy can be fostered.[49]

In order to answer these two questions, it is imperative that the curriculum designers collect both quantitative and qualitative data. Such a task should proceed in two phases. In phase one, designers can conduct something like a national survey of a representative sample of young people (both current students and recently graduated students) to obtain quantitative data on how a diverse group of young people evaluate the civics education they are receiving or have received. During this entire process, and in line with the principles of co-design, it is imperative that a select group of young people also be actively recruited and involved in the survey design and analysis. This will help ensure that youth perspectives are included and that they are not only subjects but also agents in such enquiries. As with survey participants, it is important these youth co-designers be as representative as possible with respect to gender, religion, ethnicity and socioeconomic status, with particular emphasis put on including participants beyond those who are already politically engaged. This of course remains a perennial problem—and the question of 'how' this occurs often plagues researchers in the field.

Using the survey data, investigators can then proceed to conducting focus group interviews with young people to obtain in-depth qualitative responses to the first key question. Focus groups are often useful as a way to obtain a larger number of potentially contrasting responses while enabling participants to discuss their views with each other in an intimate and unthreatening setting. Most importantly, the focus group context diminishes the power exerted by the interviewer—especially if that person is young. Again youth co-designers should not only be involved in these focus groups, but take chief responsibility in designing and running them. This will have multiple benefits, including creating a more comfortable environment for participants to speak amongst their peers and providing the chance for young people to gain research training and engagement skills.

In phase two, designers should aim to bring together a group of young people in order to form a deliberative mini-public capable of analysing and answering the second key question: how might civics education better account for young people's understandings and practices of citizenship and political participation? There is, for instance, potential here for young people to act as facilitators of deliberation[50] in the mini-public and to be the exclusive agents of a deliberative experience performed away from authority figures. This can lead, as Monique Deveaux argues, to the empowerment of subordinated members in society,[51] that is, the young, and even to young people's emancipation[52] from systemic forms of domination (e.g. exclusion from having any agency over their civics curriculum)—which could be done by feeding findings from the deliberative experience into the creation of civics education policy.[53] To inform the jurors' deliberation, the findings from phase one can be presented to act as a guide. Any such answers can be presented to relevant curriculum bodies and government agencies and form the backbone of civics curriculum design and implementation.

Of course, any co-designed civics curriculum still faces a number of potential issues and hurdles. For example, several important questions remain unanswered, including whether such designs are feasible or sustainable. As Catherine Bovill, Alison Cook-Sather and Peter Felten caution, '[i]nvolving students in designing their own education experiences can enhance student ownership of their own learning, but this implies the need for re-design by the next cohort of students to ensure that they achieve this same degree of ownership'.[54] Then there is also the matter the resulting curriculum will be affected or altered by professional standard requirements, curriculum regulatory frameworks and other political pressures within the particular country.[55] These factors may determine or at least constrain the potential and creativeness that young people can bring to the co-design table. The good news is that none of these barriers are insurmountable nor are they without policy solutions. For now, it bears restating that there is enough evidence to conclude that co-design can be an educative exercise not only for young people, but also for the educators and policymakers as well.

YOUTH PARTICIPATION AND THE DEMOCRATIC SCHOOL

Co-design is an important policy innovation that has the potential to benefit both young people and the senior policy and curriculum experts who collaborate with them on youth issues. Directly capable of influencing the communities and lived experiences of young people, the practice of co-design can therefore have a positive impact on how young people see and engage with the civics education they receive particularly when they have had a hand in its design and implementation.

There is now an extensive literature attesting to the fact that young people learn best about political participation and the idea of democracy when they have the opportunity to put it into practice within the school and their own communities.[56] As Tony Knight and Art Pearl write, 'to meaningfully learn about democracy, students must *do it*'.[57] While abstract theories are necessary, it is not until young people are empowered to exercise control over their own lives and make decisions about concerns affecting them that they will learn what it means to be a responsible citizen. What makes the school such a transformative institution is that it can either help or hinder this process.

Put differently, schools can draw on principles from the practice of co-design to encourage students into schoolwide governance boards and committees, which in many ways offers its own education in civics. For Ben Kisby and James Sloam, while 'schools cannot be fully democratic', they can certainly create opportunities that 'allow students to participate significantly in making decisions' in relation to school budgets, curriculum and other important policies.[58] What sits at the core of this proposal is the notion of constructivism: the idea that young people who have a hand in constructing their own lives are more likely to have a vested interest in seeing it succeed. In educational terms, as Cook-Sather puts it, when students become 'actors in their own learning'—that is, when they 'have opportunities to construct their learning and themselves, to develop a metacognitive awareness of those processes, and to share their experiences and insights with the adults with whom they work'—they will have taken ownership in their own education.[59] But more than this, they will have learned by doing. When it comes to something like civics education, this then has the capacity to influence their broader political behaviour and commitment beyond school boundaries.

The good news is that what we have described here is already taking place. The democratic schools movement is premised on the very idea that all those who are affected by or have a vested interest in the education system should have a right and duty to influence its production and management.[60] Inspired in part by John Dewey's argument that schools and classrooms are formative environments, the democratic schools movement thus seeks to make the school into a polity and to reframe students as citizens who are empowered to speak up, participate, deliberate, democratically contest[61] and determine matters affecting the school as a whole. The objective is to ensure that students become more than passive subjects or spectators of their own lives in the school. But with autonomy, comes responsibility. The one cannot exist without the other. This is the implicit civics lessons that the movement instils in its students: the school is only as strong as its students. The more active and engaged they are, in the various realms of the school, the more the educational experience will be enriched. Conversely, the more apathetic and disengaged the students, the more isolating and exclusive the school will become.

According to Knight and Pearl, democratic schools may not always be able to reach easy consensus or enact quick policies. But through these protracted processes, they will develop citizens who can 'propose law, policy, and practice and defend those proposals with logic and evidence in open debate'.[62] Importantly, these student-citizens will also learn to understand four fundamental cornerstones of democratic citizenship. The first is that a democratic authority, whether in school or government, is one who 'leads by persuasion and negotiation' not by edict.[63] The second cornerstone is that democracy is premised on inclusiveness. In the classroom as in society more generally, the ideal to strive for is one which values all as equal stakeholders and 'members of a problem-solving community'. The third is that there are certain rights which are inalienable, including the right of expression, the right to privacy, the right to due process and the right of movement.[64] No teacher or political authority can take these rights away. The fourth cornerstone is the importance of informed participatory decision-making. A healthy democracy is no different from a healthy democratic school in this regard: without citizens who are willing and able to exchange ideas, listen, develop coherent proposals, negotiate and compromise, rally and form parties, and keep those in positions of influence accountable, power will fall to the few rather than the many.[65]

These lessons taught in abstract may or may not hit home to students the importance of fulfilling their roles as democratic citizens in their own communities. Yet when they see its implications firsthand, through the context of participation in schoolwide governance, the idea that they *can* effect change in peaceful and meaningful ways may very well lead to instilling these virtues throughout society as students leave school, spread geographically and grow into their adult selves.

CONCLUSION

The prospect of young people co-designing curriculum with experts, for all its merits, continues to face the reality of conventional policy practices in the United Kingdom, the United States and Australia that are unwilling or unable to change. Part of the issue stems from the civic deficit perspective that certain members of the political classes in these countries hold about young people. Young people are not-yet-citizens. They are in need of training. They are people who must conform to the status quo of existing political practice. As we outline above, there appears to be little demonstrated appreciation from politicians through to curriculum experts of young people's interactive, creative, everyday and non-hierarchical political practices.

On the flipside, those politicians who *do* recognise these political attributes among the young, who may even perceive their nation's youth as fully fledged citizens with as much, or as little, political knowledge as a number of other demographic groups, are left flummoxed about how best to engage young people politically.

It should come as no surprise to the reader at this point that, from our perspective, there is at least one productive route that has not yet been given its day in court in the United Kingdom, the United States or Australia—which, of course, is putting co-design into practice. This is a route that could, firstly, help dissipate the view that young people are contributing to a civic deficit and, secondly, professionally engage a representative sample of young people in the design of civics curriculum and the politics that goes into its policy formation (if not other policy areas that are of concern to the young).

As we have shown in this chapter, practicing co-design has the potential to net the political systems using this practice a number of benefits including real-world exposure between young people and policy or curriculum experts, mutual learning, the dissipation of unhelpful stereotypes sometimes held by both parties about each another (e.g. that the young are deficient in civic virtue or that experts and politicians are out of touch with the young) and so forth. As seen in the democratic schools movement, giving young people the chance to be political enables them to enact their agency within an otherwise, if not usually, top-down hierarchical institution.

Perhaps it is time to view parliaments, political parties and the institutional machinery that make up Anglo-American democracies as but extensions of the democratic school—as places where young people can have agency, are treated with respect and are valued as partners in the quest to co-produce a civics education that might actually deliver on its promise of creating a society with civic intelligence and political nous for all.

NOTES

1. Manning, N., and K. Edwards (2014). 'Why Has Civic Education Failed to Increase Young People's Political Participation?' *Sociological Research Online* **19** (1): 1–12.

2. Bessant, J., R. Farthing, and R. Watts (2016). 'Co-designing a Civics Curriculum: Young People, Democratic Deficit and Political Renewal in the EU. *Journal of Curriculum Studies* **48** (2): 271–289.

3. O'Toole, T., D. Marsh, and S. Jones (2003). 'Political Literacy Cuts Both Ways: The Politics of Non-participation Among Young People'. *The Political Quarterly* **74** (3): 349–360, 359.

4. Gijsenbergh, J., S. Hollander, T. Houwen, and W. de Jong (eds.) (2012). *Creative Crises of Democracy.* Brussels: Peter Lang.

5. Knight, T., and A. Pearl (2000). 'Democratic Education and Critical Pedagogy'. *The Urban Review* **32** (3): 197–226.

6. Manning, and Edwards, 'Why Has Civic Education Failed to Increase Young People's Political Participation?'

7. Bessant et al. (2016). @ 275.

8. Ibid.

9. Edwards, K., L. Saha, and M. Print (2006). *Youth Electoral Study Report 3: Youth, the Family and Learning about Politics and Voting.* URL: http://www.aec.gov.au/about_aec/publications/youth_study/youth_study_3/youth_electoral_study_03.pdf. Consulted on 12 November 2015.

10. Bessant et al. (2016).

11. Ercan, S., and J.-P. Gagnon (2014). 'The Crisis of Democracy: Which Crisis? Which Democracy?' *Democratic Theory* **1** (2): 1–10.

12. Russell, A., E. Fieldhouse, K. Purdam, and V. Kalra (2002). *Voter Engagement and Young People.* London: The Electoral Commission.

13. Arvanitakis, and Marren. 'Putting the Politics Back into Politics'. E. W. Ross (2004). 'Negotiating the Politics of Citizenship Education'. *PS: Political Science and Politics* **37** (2): 249–251; J. Torney-Purta (2002). 'The School's Role in Developing Civic Engagement: A Study of Adolescents in Twenty-Eight Countries'. *Applied Developmental Science* **6** (4): 203–212.

14. Krinks, K. (1999). "Creating the Active Citizen? Recent Developments in Civics Education." *Australian Parliamentary Research Papers* **15**. URL: http://www.aph.gov.au/About_Parliament/Parliamentary_Departments/Parliamentary_Library/pubs/rp/rp9899/99RP15. Consulted on 7 June 2016.

15. Civic Expert Group (1994). *Whereas the People . . . Civics and Citizenship Education.* Canberra: AGPS, 27.

16. Ibid., 26.

17. Macintyre, S. (1995). 'An Expert's Confession'. *The Australian Quarterly* **67** (3): 1–12, 4.

18. Australian Curriculum, Assessment and Reporting Authority (2013). *Civics and Citizenship.* Sydney: ACARA.

19. Cook-Sather, A. (2010). 'Students as Learners and Teachers: Taking Responsibility, Transforming Education, and Redefining Accountability'. *Curriculum Inquiry* **40** (4): 555–575, 555.

20. Bovill, C., K. Morss, and C. J. Bulley (2009). 'Should Students Participate in Curriculum Design?' *Pedagogical Research in Maximising Education* **3** (2): 17–26.

21. See, for example: Bessell, S. (2011). 'Participation in Decision-Making in Out-of-Home Care in Australia: What Do Young People Say?' *Children and Youth Services Review* **33** (4): 496–501. @ 497; Fahmy, E. (2006). *Young Citizens: Young People's Involvement in Politics and Decision Making.* Aldershot: Ashgate. @ 21; Tisdall, K. E. M. (2008). 'Is the Honeymoon Over? Children and Young People's Participation in Public Decision-Making'. *The International Journal of Children's Rights* **16** (3): 419–429; Walker, T. (2000). 'The Service/Politics Split: Rethinking Service to Teach Political Engagement'. *PS: Political Science and Politics* **33** (3): 646–649.

22. O'Toole et al., 'Political Literacy Cuts Both Ways'. 356.

23. Head, B. (2011). 'Why Not Ask Them? Mapping and Promoting Youth Participation'. *Children and Youth Services Review* **33** (4): 541–547.

24. Briggs, L. (2011). 'Co-Design: Toward a New Service Vision for Australia?' *Public Administration Today* **25**: 35–47.

25. McCulloch, A. (2009). 'The Student as Co-producer: Learning from Public Administration about the Student-University Relationship'. *Studies in Higher Education* **34** (2): 171–183.

26. Tisdall, E. K. M., and J. Davis. (2004). 'Making a Difference? Bringing Children's and Young People's Views into Policy-Making'. *Children & Society* **18** (2): 131–142. @ 131.

27. Ibid., 36.

28. Ibid., 42.

29. Marschall, M. (2004). 'Citizen Participation and the Neighborhood Context: A New Look at the Coproduction of Local Public Goods'. *Political Research Quarterly* **57**(2): 231–244.

30. Staszowski, E., S. Brown, and B. Winter. (2013). 'Reflections on Designing for Social Innovation in the Public Sector: A Case Study of New York City'. In E. Manzini and E. Staszowski (Eds) *Public and Collaborative: Exploring the Intersection of Design, Social Innovation and Public Policy.* DESIS Network Press. pp. 27–39. @ 28.

31. Fung, A. (2006). 'Varieties of Participation in Complex Governance'. *Public Administration Review* **66** (1): 66–75.

32. Briggs, L. (2011). @ 36.

33. Fischer, F. (1993). 'Citizen Participation and the Democratization of Policy Expertise: From Theoretical Inquiry to Practical Cases'. *Policy Sciences* **26** (3): 165–187.

34. Ibid., 168.

35. Vanstone, C., and S. Schulman (2011). *Co-designing: Thriving Solutions. The Australian Centre for Social Inclusion.*

36. Collin, P., G. Lala, L. Palombo, A. Vromen, R. Marrades, and G. Maci (2016). *Creating Benefit for All: Young People, Engagement and Public Policy.* Melbourne: Young and Well Cooperative Research Centre, 9.

37. Harris, A., and J. Wyn (2010). 'Emerging Forms of Youth Participation'. *Young* **18** (1): 3–7.

38. Collin et al. (2016). @ 9.

39. Ibid., 28–29.

40. Bessant, J. (2003). 'Youth Participation: A New Model of Government'. *Policy Studies* **24** (2): 87–100, 96.

41. Head, B. (2011); Di Masi, D. and M. Santi (2016). 'Learning Democratic Thinking: A Curriculum to Philosophy for Children as Citizens'. *Journal of Curriculum Studies* **48** (1): 136–150.

42. Bessant et al. (2016).

43. Stoker, G. (2014). 'Allow Young People to Set the Political Agenda by Giving Youth Parliaments the Power to Call Referendums'. *Democratic Audit UK.* URL: http://www.democraticaudit.com/?p=5845. Consulted 6 June.

44. Healey, M., A. Flint, and K. Harrington (2014). 'Engagement through Partnership: Students as Partners in Learning and Teaching in Higher Education'. *The Higher Education Academy.* July.

45. Bovill et al. (2009).

46. Ibid., 23.

47. Ibid., 48.

48. Australian Curriculum, Assessment and Reporting Authority, *Civics and Citizenship.*

49. Ibid.

50. Moore, A. (2012). 'Following from the Front: Theorizing Deliberative Facilitation'. *Critical Policy Studies* **6** (2): 146–162.

51. Deveaux, M. (2016). 'Effective Deliberative Inclusion of Women in "Traditional" Contexts'. *Democratic Theory* **3** (2).

52. Niemeyer, S. (2011). 'The Emancipatory Effect of Deliberation: Empirical Lessons from Mini-Publics'. *Politics & Society* **39** (1): 103–140.

53. Lafont, C. (2015). 'Deliberation, Participation, and Democratic Legitimacy: Should Deliberative Mini-publics Shape Public Policy?' *The Journal of Political Philosophy* **23** (1): 40–63. We agree with Lafont, who argues that deliberative mini-publics should not be used to simply float policy recommendations, by recognizing that young peoples' mini-publics on civics education should be done in such a way that strengthens the policy cycle relationship between young people and policymakers.

54. Bovill, C., A. Cook-Sather, and P. Felten (2011). 'Students as Co-creators of Teaching Approaches, Course Design, and Curricula: Implications for Academic Developers'. *International Journal for Academic Development* **16** (2): 133–145, 142.

55. Bovill et al. (2009).

56. Torney-Purta, J. (2002). 'The School's Role in Developing Civic Engagement: A Study of Adolescents in Twenty-Eight Countries'. *Applied Developmental Science* **6** (4): 203–212.

57. Knight and Pearl, 'Democratic Education and Critical Pedagogy', 200.

58. Kisby, B., and J. Sloam (2012). 'Citizenship, Democracy and Education in the UK: Towards a Common Framework for Citizenship Lessons in the Four Home Nations'. *Parliamentary Affairs* **65** (1): 68–89.

59. Cook-Sather (2010). @ 560–561.

60. Ibid.

61. Giroux, H. (2014). 'The Swindle of Democracy in the Neoliberal University and the Responsibility of Intellectuals'. *Democratic Theory* **1** (1): 9–37.

62. Knight and Pearl (2000). @ 203.

63. Ibid., 206.

64. Ibid., 211.

65. Ibid., 213–214.

Index

About the Authors

Mark Chou is Associate Professor of Politics at the Australian Catholic University.

Jean-Paul Gagnon is Associate Professor of Politics at the University of Canberra.

Catherine Hartung is Lecturer in Education Studies at the University of Otago.

Lesley J. Pruitt is Senior Lecturer in Politics and International Relations at Monash University.